D0938966

The
CONDUCTOR'S
Legacy

The CONDUCTOR'S *Legacy*

CONDUCTORS ON CONDUCTING FOR WIND BAND

Frank Battisti

Harry Begian

Col. John Bourgeois

Ray E. Cramer

James Croft

Col. Arnald Gabriel

H. Robert Reynolds

Richard Strange

David Whitwell

COMPILED AND EDITED BY PAULA A. CRIDER

FOREWORD BY JERRY F. JUNKIN

GIA Publications, Inc.
Chicago

The Conductor's Legacy
Frank Battisti, Col. John Bourgeois, Ray E. Cramer, James Croft,
Col. Arnald Gabriel, H. Robert Reynolds, Richard Strange, and
David Whitwell. Foreword by Jerry F. Junkin. Compiled and
edited by Paula A. Crider.

G-7660
ISBN: 978-1-57999-752-6

Copyright © 2010 GIA Publications, Inc.
7404 S Mason Ave
Chicago IL 60638

www.giamusic.com

Lovingly dedicated to Frederick Fennell, whose life had a profound effect upon the evolution of wind bands and wind literature.

CONTENTS

FOREWORD
Jerry F. Junkin

The Conductor's Legacy is a wonderful collection of interviews with the leading band conductors of our time. Frank Battisti, Harry Begian, John Bourgeois, Jim Croft, Ray Cramer, Arnald Gabriel, H. Robert Reynolds, Richard Strange, and David Whitwell have all served as great models for our profession for well over half a century. The number of musicians fortunate to have performed under their leadership is remarkable in and of itself. However, it is the deep musicianship that each of these extraordinary personalities exude that makes them and their music making so very special.

Paula Crider has interviewed each of these wonderful conductors and compiled the results into what has become this book. Undoubtedly, *The Conductor's Legacy* will be used as a reference tool for current and future generations of band conductors. These gentlemen have changed the landscape of our profession. We owe them all a great debt of gratitude for their efforts to place the band medium firmly into the mainstream of the world of music. Never satisfied with the status quo, these musicians of the highest order continue to push forward the boundaries of bands and band music.

We are indeed also fortunate that Paula Crider has been able to capture their stories—stories that needed to be told—for all of us. I can't imagine a better person to do this than Paula, whose remarkable insight and clarity of thought comes through in the probing questions that generate each interview. Paula Crider's career has had an incredible impact on our profession. Always a leader, her presidencies of such organizations as the National Band Association and the American Bandmasters Association have forever changed the world of music and bands. I cannot imagine a better person to have taken on this project, and no one could have done it as well.

As we consider the past century encompassed by the stories of these gifted musicians, it falls to each of us to consider where we will go from this point. These are stories of talent, work, sacrifice, ingenuity, bravery, and determination. These leaders of our profession remind us not only of where we have come from, but provide an inspirational handoff to us and to future generations. It is up to us to continue to move the profession forward, to be champions of our medium, and to always work to be the kind of inspirational musicians, teachers, and leaders that Battisti, Begian, Bourgeois, Croft, Cramer, Gabriel, Reynolds, Strange, and Whitwell have been. While it might not be possible, what comes through in the pages of *The Conductor's Legacy* is that it is the journey for each of us that is so joyous and ultimately, rewarding.

—*Jerry F. Junkin*, Director of Bands
The University of Texas at Austin

PREFACE

Every generation of human endeavor is blessed with those visionary leaders who teach by example and serve as a source of inspiration for all who are fortunate to profit through association, no matter how tangential. These leaders, in retrospect, change our worlds, and in so doing elevate our art and nurture and challenge the creative spirit within.

Once outside the box, their individual journeys may take widely divergent paths, but one thread of commonality is apparent in all: they each seem to possess an uncommon desire to reach ever deeper levels of musical understanding and they exude a passion for conveying the inexpressible through the medium of music.

What makes these leaders exceptional? Why are they not satisfied to dwell in that gray twilight of mediocrity that so often characterizes our profession? The answers lie within the fabric of lives rich with experience, lives built upon a solid foundation of knowledge gleaned through insatiable curiosity and a relentless pursuit of that ever-elusive state of musical perfection.

In 2004 I enjoyed the privilege of hosting Frederick Fennell when he served as Master Mentor at the National Band Association Young Conductor, Young Composer Mentor Project held at Illinois State University. It was there that the impetus for this book was born with Maestro Fennell's inimitably enthusiastic endorsement. The need for such a sharing of knowledge became apparent as Fred spoke of his personal conversations with Percy Grainger and of his eternal regret that he did not encourage Grainger to put pen to paper as have the conductors in this book.

With Frederick Fennell's indefatigable enthusiasm and cogent suggestions, a series of questions were formulated to provide the next generation of conductors with a wealth of insights. My one great regret is that the man whose vision changed the world of wind bands did not live to complete his own interview for this book.

I am extremely grateful to the legendary conductors who so generously shared their time and talents. Some contributed their thoughts during personal interviews; others graciously took the time to answer questions via email. All are truly remarkable men whose effect upon bands and band music has shaped the wind band world in a most positive and lasting manner. By sharing their life stories, knowledge, and passion for music, they will also influence many generations to come.

—*Paula A. Crider*

Note that questions not answered by
the conductors featured here are omitted.

Chapter 1

FRANK BATTISTI

How did you begin your musical journey? Who were your first teachers and sources of inspiration?

My musical journey began at Inlet Valley School, a two-room country school south of Ithaca, NY. George Hathaway was my general music teacher. He visited our school once a week and led us in the singing of familiar songs and taught us basic musical skills. He also gave lessons to students who wanted to play an instrument.

I started studying the cornet when I was in fifth grade. Students in those days (1940s) played the cornet, not the trumpet. Mr. Hathaway was a very good teacher. He was energetic, supportive, and encouraging. After studying with him for a year, he recommended that I take lessons with the

Ithaca High School band director, Joseph Rossina.

During my last year at Inlet Valley School I took a school bus into Ithaca every Monday afternoon, got off at the high school, and made my way to Mr. Rossina's office for my lesson. It was a bit scary walking down corridors filled with what seemed like very big high school students to get to Mr. Rossina's office!

Netti Lawrence, my fourth, fifth, and sixth grade teacher, was a *fantastic* woman, teacher, and role model. She seemed to know everything. Mrs. Lawrence had high expectations for all of us and did whatever was necessary to make sure we achieved them.

I began attending concerts by the Ithaca College Concert Band, conducted by Walter Beeler, in 1946. The band was terrific. It was made up of former World War II service band musicians. Once I had heard this band perform I knew I wanted to become a band director.

Were there any conductors who made a lasting impression on you during your early years?

There were three professional orchestra conductors, three wind band/ensemble conductors, and one composer who influenced me as a young band director.

Band Directors and Conductors

In the 1950s and 60s, Frederick Fennell became an important role model for me. I was inspired by his conducting and his ideas and vision about wind groups (wind ensemble). I started to travel to Rochester, NY in 1960 (with my Ithaca High School Band members) to attend concerts he conducted with the Eastman Wind Ensemble. They were a great inspiration for all of us. Fred guest-conducted my Ithaca High

School Band every year from 1960–67.

Walter Beeler taught me how to achieve a beautiful wind-band tone. Walt's Ithaca College Bands always played with wonderful clarity and a warm, resonant tone.

I admired William D. Revelli not only for the wonderful performances he produced with the University of Michigan Symphony Band, but also for his lifelong commitment and contributions to the American school band movement.

Professional Orchestra Conductors

Listening to performances on the radio in the 1940s and 50s played a major role in the development of my love of music. Artuo Toscanini's Saturday night broadcast concerts with the NBC Symphony Orchestra thrilled and inspired me. I loved the passion he brought to his music making.

Bruno Walter also conducted wonderful broadcast performances with the New York Philharmonic and Metropolitan Opera. Because I lived in Ithaca I was able to hear live concerts by the Cleveland Orchestra conducted by George Szell every year (for twenty years) at Cornell University's Bailey Hall. I marveled at Szell's control over the orchestra and his elegant performances.

Composer

Warren Benson was the most influential person in my life. His knowledge and ideas about music and creativity excited and inspired me. He continually challenged me to learn more. As a result I became a better musician, teacher, and conductor.

If you could begin your college years all over again, would you do anything differently?

No. I received a *great* education at Ithaca College! I performed wonderful music in the college orchestra, band, and choir. My choral experiences helped me become a better instrumentalist. All my teachers were demanding, encouraging, and supportive. The Ithaca College music education curriculum placed great emphasis on every student's musical development.

What advice can you offer to current music majors or young band directors?

Seek out and study with the best artists and scholars; observe master conductors and teachers. Consume great literature, art, and music.

What were your early years of teaching like? What memories or lessons learned can you share?

I was constantly frustrated during my first years of teaching. I felt like quitting every other day. I knew what I wanted to achieve, but I couldn't make it happen quickly. Fortunately, a veteran teacher offered me some excellent advice. He told me to work hard and exercise patience: "It will take time to develop an excellent music education band program." This advice proved to be right. I stayed at Ithaca High School for fourteen years and the New England Conservatory for thirty years.

How do you structure your rehearsals?

After tuning, I rehearse selected passages from the music. Once I'm satisfied with the progress we've made, I conduct the players through the section of the work containing these passages so they will understand how they fit into the context of the music. I never exceed the time allocated in the rehearsal schedule for a piece, and I don't play through a work until one or two rehearsals before a performance.

How do you approach score study?

I start studying a score well in advance of the time I have to conduct the piece (ideally, about six months in advance). This gives me time to live with and to absorb the score in a non-pressured way. I view score study as an informative and enlightening dialogue between the composer and myself.

I begin with readings of the score (no stops), giving free reign to my intuition and imagination. I try to get a feeling for the form and expressiveness of the piece prior to analyzing its musical components. My interpretation (perception of the piece's character, meaning, and spirit) is an amalgamation of my subjective feelings and intellectual understanding of the anatomy of the piece.

What is your concept of band sound? How do you achieve it?

I try to create the sound/tone appropriate for the style and expressive character of the piece. Wagner's *Trauersinfonie* requires a completely different kind of tone than does John Harbison's *Three City Blocks*. All ensemble tone, regardless of its style, should be resonant and well balanced.

What are your views on score marking?

I put many markings in my scores. Score markings help me to better remember things. If time permitted, I would hand-copy every score I studied. Doing this would ensure that I saw and considered all the score's details.

How can we best advance our art?

All young people need to have opportunities to consume, create, and re-create music. Performing good quality music in small and large ensembles provides excellent opportunities for young (and older) people to experience the awesome expressive power of music.

In order to create a society of music lovers, music education programs need to help young students develop an understanding and appreciation of music. Band program experiences often consist of too much activity and not enough art.

It's important that band music education focus on the development of every student's musical potential.

What works did you program on your farewell concert?

I really had two farewell concerts: one as Director of the Ithaca (NY) High School Band and the other as conductor of the New England Conservatory Wind Ensemble.

My farewell concert with the Ithaca High School Band on May 17, 1967, consisted of the following works:

Herbert Bielawa	*Prisms*
Vincent Persichetti	*Turn Not Thy Face*
David Borden	*All-American Teenage Lovesongs*
Robert Ward	*Fiesta Processional*
Warren Benson	*Helix*
Percy Grainger	*Lincolnshire Posy*
Warren Benson	*Leaves Are Falling*

My final concert with the New England Conservatory Wind Ensemble on April 15, 1999, included:

Henry Purcell/ Steven Stucky	*Funeral Music for Queen Mary*
Igor Stravinsky	*Octet for Wind Instruments*
Henk Badings	*Concerto for Flute and Wind Orchestra*
Gustav Holst	*Hammersmith,* op. 52

| Alan Fletcher | *An American Song* |
| Gunther Schuller | *On Winged Flight (Divertimento for Band)* |

What are your current sources of inspiration or spiritual enrichment?

My family, friends, and faith are great sources of inspiration for me. I read the bible every day. I also read poetry, history, autobiographies, and biographies. The time I spend outdoors and listening to great artists perform always enriches my soul and charges my batteries.

What are your interests beyond music?

I love history, sports (especially baseball and the Boston Red Sox), travel, and reading. I also enjoy taking my wife, Charlotte out for coffee every afternoon I'm home.

To what do you attribute your exceptional musical success?

I have a great love of music and a passion for sharing it with others. This compels me to work hard and strive to become a better person, musician, conductor, and teacher.

If you could do it all over again, would you do anything differently?

I would develop better piano technique, develop stronger basic musicianship skills (inner hearing), and conduct choral and orchestral music.

How would you like your epitaph to read?

I think I would borrow a quote by Donald Hall (United States Poet Laureate, 2007): "(His) gift to students was not information but demonstration of engagement."

Any final thoughts or words of advice?

Conductors play a very important role in the intertwining composer-interpreter relationship. We are responsible for presenting the composer's creative work to the public. To carry out this responsibility, conductors must have a commanding presence and a passion for music, a fabulous memory, imagination, and excellent leadership skills, as well as the deftness of a psychologist, teacher, organizer, and a fount of inspiration.

Chapter 2

HARRY BEGIAN

How did you begin your musical journey? Who were your first teachers and sources of inspiration?

My parents were immigrants who survived the exile of Armenians from Turkey. My father came to America first and found a job with the idea of sending back for families. My grandfather was a priest and schoolmaster in a community of 4.000 Armenians. My Mother and sister stayed behind and were sent on a horrifying march on foot to Lebanon across the Mesopotamian desert. My Mother survived, but she lost her daughter. This was the first genocide of the twentieth century.

The horrors of this genocide were told to me, and it has affected my life deeply. My family was treated like animals.

My dad was in Massachusetts, and earned enough money to bring my mother over, but were it not for the American Red Cross, he would never have found her again. They were separated for seven years. I was born on April 24, 1921. Coincidentally, April 24 was the same date that Armenians were sent into exile several years before my birth.

It wasn't easy assimilating. I didn't know a word of English when I began first grade. I started music in the fourth grade. I was handed a dirty, beat-up Conn cornet and a fingering chart, and was pretty much left on my own as to how to play the instrument.

My first method book was the H. A. Vandercook book. My first band director was Joseph Godfrey. At my tender age, my first band director was a hero. I found that I was almost by nature a very good sight reader, and later learned much more from his brother, T. P. Godfrey, who was my high school band director. I used to play trumpet duets with him and he helped me along. I never had a private lesson until I got to the university where I studied with Leonard Smith.

I fell in love with music in general when I heard the Detroit Symphony Orchestra *Concerts for Children*. I was taken to a concert when I was in junior high school. This was the first time I heard a symphony orchestra and I was just amazed by the sound. I fell in love with classical music from way back and it never left me.

Were there any conductors who made a lasting impression on you during your early years?
Yes, I first heard the Michigan band under Revelli about 1935–36, when I was still in high school. This was the first time I realized that a band could be a refined musical instrument. The other thing that created interest was when I first

heard Leonard Falcone solo on a high school band concert. I had never heard solo playing like that. He played "O Solo Mio" as an encore, and I thought, "Ah, that's what they mean about espressivo!" Leonard Smith was my trumpet teacher. His big thing was accuracy, and he taught me to play with great technical accuracy and dynamic control.

Larry Teal was a tremendous influence in my life. When I began teaching at Cass Technical High School in Detroit, he became my mentor. I studied saxophone and also flute. I was pretty much of a roughneck. My parents didn't approve of my concentrating on music. In their culture they valued doctor, lawyer, engineer.

Larry Teal took a personal interest in me. He was one of the finest musicians, philosophers, and teachers I ever knew. When my Cass Tech band played at The Midwest Clinic and received a thunderous reception, Larry Teal told me that I needed to go to a university and get my doctorate (the union card of college band directors) so that I could have a college position. Teal felt so strongly about this that he actually volunteered to pay for my return to college, but I had enough saved up to attend the University of Michigan.

If you could begin your college years all over again, would you do anything differently?

I originally wanted to be an orchestra conductor, but reality struck at the age of fifteen or sixteen when I realized that I needed a good piano background. My parents couldn't afford to have me take piano lessons when I was younger, so I should have made it a priority to learn to play piano while a college student.

What advice can you offer to current music majors or young band directors?

First of all, make sure that if you're going to be a conductor that you carefully choose a school where the band director and the teacher on your instrument are of the top order. So many pick a school because of a private teacher and land in a school band playing for someone who is less than good. Go to a school that has the best.

What were your early years of teaching like? What memories or lessons learned can you share?

When I was sixteen years old, the director of the Boys Club asked me to form a band. I was paid $15.00 a month, and I recruited and formed a band of about twenty-five players. I learned to select good music. I had to be shrewd because we had very little music.

As a student conductor at Wayne State, I learned to establish some breathing room between the players and myself. If you're going to be in a position of leadership, you have to have control of the rehearsals.

When I went to Cass Tech, I was kind of a disciplinarian. It took some years to back off and learn that students want to be addressed by their names, and that I didn't have to raise my voice. (I used to speak rather loudly—I was frightening!)

I learned that I had to work hard as a conductor and teacher and demand the same of my players in return. I wanted my players to come to the point where we could experience joy. I asked my students to work hard. The joy we get out of serious playing is what we should be working for.

How do you structure your rehearsals?

My librarian would put up the order on a chalk board. After that, the first clarinet sounded the pitch. We couldn't afford a

Strobotuner[1], but maybe that was a good thing. All I had was
a tuning bar and my ears. Before I came into the band hall,
the first pitch would be sounded, then I would enter and we
would play a Bach chorale—not the one in F; too many play
just that one.

After the chorale, we would listen for attacks, releases,
play slight *accelerandos* and *ritardandos* to focus attention
on what I was asking of them. If that was satisfactory, then
get on to the first piece, usually of a spirited nature.

Next came the most difficult piece. My high school class
period was only forty-five minutes, so the rehearsal plan had
to be well thought out. I had to have an idea in mind. I was
forced to learn to plan time well and know what I could
accomplish in limited rehearsal time.

Before a concert we would have Wednesday afternoon
one-hour rehearsals. I would always end rehearsals with a
number that I knew they particularly enjoyed.

How do you approach score study?

First, I would take a score that my sense of discrimination
told me was a worthwhile piece of music, that my band could
play, and I could teach them. I spent a lot of time at home or
at my office to go through the score from beginning to end. I
don't have piano capabilities, so I would solfège the score. I
learned this in my lessons with Leonard Smith, and later took
solfège lessons at Tanglewood. (This reminds me of two other
sources of inspiration: the Boston Symphony under Sergei
Koussevitzky, and Robert Shaw. I sang in Shaw's chorale.)

Beethoven's *Ninth* and the Dvorak *Requiem*—that's where

---

1   An electronic instrument giving an accurate visual indication of the frequency of a
    sound or an electrical signal. It compares the frequency to be measured with internal
    frequency standards based upon the equally tempered musical scale but can be used to
    measure frequencies in any scale.

I learned that the conductor has to sweat before he can expect any kind of work from singers and players. If the conductor doesn't give out energy, he can't expect energy from players. Koussevitzky had the worst singing voice, but he would always sing for the BSO. That's the way the big boys do it. That's the way I wanted to do it!

What is your concept of band sound? How do you achieve it?

I really loved it when I became *the* band director and could develop the sound that I think a band should make. As I listened to great bands and orchestras, I realized that there were certain qualities other than the persons in the ensemble affecting band sound. The total size of the organization divided by the number of players in each section as well as the dynamics of the mix between the various sections, all contribute to overall sonority.

When I heard the wonderful Revelli sound, I wanted to know how he got a sound that was so breezy, so refined, with a beautiful quality in all registers and a balance in all sections. I noticed that the size was roughly ninety players, and I thought, "Hey, that's the size of a symphony orchestra!"

I like a band with clarinets making the largest section because that is the basic sound of the band. Here's a rundown of my ideal band:

B-flat clarinet	20
Flute	a pretty large section to extend the clarinet section into the clarion register
Oboe	2
English horn	1
Saxophone	One on a part
Bass clarinet	3

Contrabass clarinet

E-flat	1
B-flat	1
Bassoon	2
Contrabassoon	1
Cornet	2–2–2
Trumpet	1–1
Horn in F	8
Trombone	2–2–2
Euphonium	4
Tuba	4
String bass	2
Percussion	at least 6

And finally, the thing no one seems to talk about is the importance of seating. Band seating also affects band sound. I experimented at Cass Tech until I got the sound that I wanted.

I don't subscribe to a wind ensemble sound that is more geared to the brasses. When you can't hear the flute, then you've got the wrong kind of band—too much debris! I object to that kind of balance.

What are your views on score marking?

I marked my scores with a number one pencil. Why number one? So that I could erase it later. I didn't use colored pencils or anything of that sort, because, to me, that was like a defacement of the score.

What works did you program on your farewell concert?

I don't remember specifically, but I always loved playing the great works: Grainger's *Lincolnshire Posy,* Hindemith...all the great works for winds, original or transcriptions. I love Elgar's *Enigma Variations.*

What are your current sources of inspiration or spiritual enrichment?

Well, I read; I listen. Future band conductors should go to all the concerts they can. They should go to all the conventions that they can attend. They should listen closely to what they hear. Compare what they see on the podium. Accept the good, and reject the things that are not so good in what they hear and what they see. Then read, read, read—all kinds of subjects on music, on history, on performance practices. Hear music that is played well.

A conductor can't ever read too much. My greatest discovery as a kid was the public library. I could check out all the books that I wanted. Later, at university, the Detroit Public Library was across the street. It had the greatest score and record collection. The first symphony orchestra I conducted was the Boston Symphony Orchestra. I set up a wire stand with score and a broken baton, and conducted Wagner's *Die Meistersinger von Nürnberg.*

What are your interests beyond music?

I read world history, biographies, and sometimes politics.

To what do you attribute your exceptional musical success?

I find that question really hard to answer.

I couldn't even write my own biography. I had to ask John Locke to do it for me. Any success that I might have had came from always making a point to hear and to see fine groups (and not so fine groups); fine conductors (and not so fine conductors). I learned from them all.

As a youngster, I used to sneak into Detroit Symphony rehearsals. I wanted to see how the pros operated. That's how I learned about rehearsals, and how to treat players, and how to make requests of players. The basic thing I learned was that they all treated music very seriously. I tried to learn as much as I could about the music so that I could give my best as a teacher to the players and then demand their best of the music. I gave my best to the music, and therefore I had a right to expect that my band would give their best to the music.

Any final thoughts or words of advice?

Be careful to exercise your tastes in choosing music, Be very discriminating musically, and don't just play what other band directors are playing. You chose the music. Let it be something that you think is worthy of the time you will spend in learning it.

Don't play cheap quality and stuff for immediate consumption. Always consider the players, and what they are playing, and what effect it will have on them and ultimately on the audience.

Don't leave the audience out in the rain. Don't force-feed them, and don't just play music that you and your colleagues are interested in. Exercise your musical judgment.

Chapter 3
COL. JOHN BOURGEOIS

How did you begin your musical journey? Who were your first teachers and sources of inspiration?

I was the product of an itinerant Music Man. I lived in a very rural area of Southwest Louisiana in the town of Gibson, on the banks of Bayou Black. This small town, with fewer than 100 people, had a post office, a general store, an elementary school, and a meeting hall. It was here that I encountered Mr. Campbell, with his satchel of wares. I started third grade on a tonette, then I played clarinet, and then cornet. I then moved across the river where I attended St. Charles Boromeo Elementary.

Father Basti sent me to Destrihan High School to take lessons because my school didn't have a music program. We then moved to Metarie, Louisiana, where I re-encountered Mr. Campbell and his Campbell School of Music. I resumed lessons, and often on Saturdays I would march in little parades wearing a blue cape with the CSM logo emblazoned in gold on the back.

I attended Jesuit High School in New Orleans, where Mr. Campbell had been appointed to be the new band director. He was soon removed (due to incompetence, I'm sure) but then I met one of the great influences of my life: the new band director, Salvatore Castigliola. I took lessons with Mr. Castigliola, and he suggested that I take up the French horn. I was principal horn because I was the only horn at the time!

I then took private lessons from an old Italian horn player, Mr. Orso. The lessons consisted of about twenty minutes of solfège, and then the horn. He would spank students who were not prepared for their lessons. I went on to study with Richard Macke and Myron Bloom, both of whom were in the New Orleans Philharmonic at the time.

In my senior year at Jesuit High I got to travel out of the state for the very first time. It was a band trip to sunny Florida. Mr. Cas had become ill and asked me to take the band. I wrote the drill and formation for the halftime show, which featured a swaying palm tree as the band played "Bali Hai." So here we were in tropical Pensacola, and the temperature was thirty-six degrees; one of the coldest days of my life!

I then attended Loyola University in New Orleans, where I studied with Vincent Orso and Bob Elworthy. Bob was a great teacher who stressed sound projection through the proper use of hand position. He later went to Indiana as a protégé of Phil Fracas.

In 1956 I was going to be drafted, so I enlisted in the Marine Corps. I went to basic training in San Diego. At the end of basic training, I was named one of three to be advanced to Pfc. When the Drill Instructor named the three, he said, "Bourgeois, you might keep good notes, but personally, I don't think you march for s___!" Such was life in the Marines.

> [At this point in the interview, Col. Bourgeois quickly recited the ten-step procedure for firing the M1 rifle: IAMUWEECAT.—Ed.]

Boot camp was difficult and was meant to be demeaning, but it was nothing compared to the rigors of infantry training at Camp Pendleton. After infantry training, I was assigned to the Marine Band Department of the Pacific at Treasure Island in San Francisco, where I became principal hornist. I was stationed in San Francisco from 1957 to 1958, then I won the audition for "The President's Own" Marine Band in Washington DC in July of 1958.

Were there any conductors who made a lasting impression on you during your early years?
Castigliola exuded a love of music and transferred that onto me while I was in high school. Mr. Cas had been the principal trumpet player of the Sanger Theater Orchestra, where overtures, opera highlights, and light classical music was used for accompanying silent movies, so it was overtures, operatic *potpourris,* and symphonic movements that we played in high school—no popular music whatsoever.

I remember one program in particular: *Overture to Oberon,* Faust's *Fantasie,* "Andante Cantabile" from Tchaikovsky's *Symphony no. 5,* "Nocturne" from Mendelssohn's *Midsummer Night's Dream,* and Wagner's Overture to *Reinzi.* This literature set my goals as a struggling horn player! The experience of playing only great music provided a firm musical foundation for me, and I shall always be grateful to Mr. Cas.

My college director, George Jansen, was a great influence in instilling wind band repertoire and style. He played trumpet in the West Point Band and came to New Orleans where he played with the Philharmonic and the Opera. He was a master teacher who, when I was director of the Marine Band, sent me a tape of his fifteen-year old student, Wynton Marsalis, who played as brilliantly then as he does today.

Others I admired in New Orleans were: the wonderful Italian conductor of the New Orleans Opera, Renato Cellini, and conductors of the Philharmonic, Massimo Freccia and Alexander Hillsberg.

As a student I ushered for the Community Concert Series where I heard Arturo Toscanni and the NBC Orchestra on tour in a performance of Tchaikovsky's *Manfred* Symphony, and Leopold Stokowski conducting a performance of Debussy's *Nocturnes.* These performances were held in the old Municipal Auditorium, which could be divided into two performance areas. The Stokowski performance took place during Mardi Gras, and the other side of the auditorium was used for a Mardi Gras ball. As Stokowski was in the middle of *Fetes,* and during the sudden *subito piano* prior to the muted trumpet entrance, the *Grand March from Aida* could be heard through the back wall. Stokowski stopped the orchestra, turned around to the audience and said, "New Orleans is a wonderful city. It's the only place in the world where you can hear two concerts for the price of one!" He turned back to the orchestra and concluded the performance.

While a student at Loyola, I became a backstage conductor for Cellini and the New Orleans Opera. I remember a dress rehearsal of *Lame.* It was a dark forest scene, and I was peering through the knothole of a tree, attempting to see the conductor in the pit while conducting a back-stage element of chorus, horns and harmonium. Leaning too far forward, I fell through the set and landed on stage!

My more recent mentors have been my Marine Band predecessors: Santlemann, Schoepper, Harpham, and Kline. My personal conducting idol is Pierre Boulez. Talk about sculpting a monument with the smallest of gestures...that's my ideal. I was mesmerized when I first saw him conduct. No extraneous gestures whatsoever; nothing to interfere with the music.

If you could begin your college years all over again, would you do anything differently?

I was very much an introvert before I went to college. In my senior year of high school, one of my Jesuit teachers advised that I should be involved in something in addition to band. With his coaching, I auditioned and was accepted into the Philatelic Society. Jesuit High was an all-male school, and in those days only performed the Shakespeare plays. I auditioned and won one of the comic roles in *Twelfth Night*. As a result of my stage involvement, my introverted cocoon hatched into an extraverted butterfly.

I joined everything at Loyola. I was freshman class president, music school reporter for the paper, and pledged two fraternities: ADG (a social organization) and professional music fraternity Phi Mu Alpha Sinfonia. I joined the Loyola Thespians and performed in many great roles. I acted in the French Quarter's Gallery Circle Theater, and I earned tuition by managing the concession stand for a large drive-in movie theater. However, school-wise, I should have applied myself more rather than just enjoying my role as a college student.

What advice can you offer to current music majors or young band directors?

Apply yourself. Be diverse; go beyond the book; investigate.

I loved overtures, surely as the result of Mr. Cas' influenced. I probably had every overture recorded on 78 rpm recordings. One of the most treasured recordings other than overtures was the tomb scene from *Aida* with Rosa Ponselle and Giovanni Martinelli. I thought it was the most beautiful thing I had ever heard in my life.

My family had no musical background whatsoever. My father hoped I would go into something like petroleum engineering. He loved classic Dixieland, and my mother used to listen to some of my overtures. She especially loved *Rienzi*.

My advice? Listen to great music!

How do you structure your rehearsals?

As director of the Marine Band, and not having been a pedagogue, obviously you don't teach notes. While performing two concerts a week with a different program every week, rehearsal time is extremely limited. The musicians check out the music in advance and come to rehearsal prepared. The challenge is in putting it all together; balancing, interpreting, and hopefully making music.

How do you approach score study?

Generally, mine is a fast study. There is so much music to cover and so little time. I do a quick architectural study: tempo relationships, technical problems, etc. The most difficult thing for me is accompanying soloists (often two per week). One must take care to observe the many *rubatos*, *accelerandos*, etc.

What is your concept of band sound? How do you achieve it?

My conception of a band's sound comes from the instrument that I inherited, The United States Marine Band. If we investigate what that sound is, I think the answer lies in the instrumentation and the balance of instruments employed— basically, the use of cornets and trumpets where indicated. To my ear there is a distinct difference in tone color of an ensemble where only trumpets are used.

Also increasing rather than diminishing of the number of woodwinds used to balance the brass. I heartily endorse the wind ensemble approach, but only with the repertoire and numbers for which the piece was written. For example, I find it ludicrous when I hear Hindemith's Symphony in B-flat played with a decimated ensemble employing only trumpets. The same goes for the Schoenberg *Theme and Variations, op. 43a* using only trumpets!

What are your views on score marking?

I mark my scores for older eyes now. I mark time, key, and tempo changes, though not in color. I mark dynamics and rehearsal numbers or letters. I'll also mark and number phrases, intensity and balances, and indicate whatever cues are needed.

How can we best advance our art?

I believe and encourage investment in the future by supporting the commissioning of new literature for our medium, but we tend to neglect our glorious heritage from the past. Somehow or other the performances of marches has become *de classe*. We are losing audiences. I wonder if there might be a connection?

What works did you program on your farewell concert?

I would include one of my favorite pieces, *The Solitary Dancer*, Warren Benson's miniature masterpiece. I love that piece!

Maybe the Berlioz Symphony *Funebre et Triomphale*. Probably one of the most neglected pieces in the repertoire because of its demanding tessitura and length.

Obviously some Wagner: *Elsa's Procession, Forest Murmurs*. I once was a guest on *Desert Island Disc,* and had to pick a program of music to take to my island. Here are my choices:

W. A. Mozart	*Gran Partita* (Serenade no. 10 in B-flat Major for Winds), K.361
	"Dove sono i bei moment" from *Le nozzle di Figaro*, K. 492, Kiri Te Kanawa, soprano
Richard Wagner	*Siegfried Idyll*, WWV 103
Giuseppe Verdi	any overture
John Philip Sousa	any march

Actually, I had two farewell concerts with the Marine Band. The first was my final orchestra concert:

W. A. Mozart	Overture to *Don Giovanni*, K.527
F. J. Haydn	Symphony no. 31 (*Hornsignal*) H I 31
Robert Schumann	*Konzertstuck* for Four Horns and Orchestra, op. 86
	Symphony no. 8 in B Minor (*Unfinished.*), D. 759

My final Marine Band concert was at my retirement and change of command, for which I arranged "Elsa's Procession" with the big ending featuring organ and trumpets as it appears at the end of the second act of *Lohengrin*.

What are your current sources of inspiration or spiritual enrichment?

A good cabernet or martini. I love to invoke the spirits!

What are your interests beyond music?

Building, gardening, cooking, being with friends.

To what do you attribute your exceptional musical success?

While I was director of the Marine Band, Tim Foley and I sought to resolve what we perceived to be a problem in identifying future leadership and conductors. We decided to write a syllabus for someone who would be assistant director, and eventually director of "The President's Own." Like musicians everywhere, they would complain, "Why don't we play this?" or, "You're playing veal and we wanted roast beef." So we asked each potential candidate to submit programs for:

A spring concert series

A summer concert series

A state dinner for X

A chamber music program

Additionally, we required a list of what would be needed in terms of instrumentation, how much time would be needed for rehearsal, etc. We waited with great anticipation, and were given some of the most bizarre lists ever seen. With each person, we could tell with whom they had studied. The most evident aspect was that they had not grown at all. There was nothing new, and no sign of their having investigated literature that they had not performed.

The key is to use other people's programs as a resource. To think, "Oh, I'd forgotten that piece," or "I didn't know

X composer wrote that." One of the reasons we instituted the Marine Band Newsletter was to list programs in order to let people know what we were programming and how that might be of service to other directors.

Any final thoughts or words of advice?
Go beyond Groves; find catalogs; go digging for good music. Be inquisitive; look in libraries. There are many treasures to be found.

Chapter 4
RAY E. CRAMER

How did you begin your musical journey? Who were your first teachers and sources of inspiration?

Growing up on a farm in west central Illinois with no music of any kind in our home other than a few pop 78s that my sisters played on a crank Victrola gave me little chance to have any kind of musical background. I attended a two-room rural schoolhouse with grades 1–3 in one room and 4–6 in the other. During my sixth-grade year a music teacher visited our school to show us several of the wind instruments and actually played a few to elicit some interest in us to play an instrument. I was lured by the glamour of a glissando on the trombone, and since no one else had chosen that instrument, I could be first chair!

When I discovered there was the expectation to practice, the glamour of the glissando quickly faded. It was cutting into my having fun time with my friends. So, like many who have traveled down this path, I quit. This did not make my father very happy, as he had to sell a couple of hogs to buy the trombone which now was gathering dust in the back of my bedroom.

In the summer before my transition to junior high school there was a knock on our front door. To our surprise the new band director in our district introduced himself and directly got to the question of why I had not signed up for junior high band. I tried to share several reasons I had decided to drop band: I did not want to practice, it would cut into all the athletic things I wanted to do, I was a terrible player, etc., etc.

The new band director's name was Don Zimmerman. He talked with my parents, asked me if I would like to hear him play trombone, and could he give me a short lesson right then? He assured me I would have a really fun time playing in his band. He proceeded to get his personal trombone out of his car and played some fantastic music that sounded like no trombone sound I had ever made. He asked me to get my horn and he gave me a thirty-minute lesson. When the lesson was over I was sounding better than I ever had. He told my parents he would give me a private lesson once a week at no cost if they would just make the effort of picking me up late from school or bringing me to town on Saturday. We only lived seven miles out of town, so my mom agreed right away to this arrangement.

Mr. Zimmerman was such an inspiration to me. His lessons were positive and productive. He challenged me every week to strive for new goals. I could not practice enough as I relished the challenge. If the weather was fairly warm, my father directed me to practice outdoors or in the barn, which gave him some relief from hearing me practice all the time, but egg production dropped off dramatically!

As funny and true as this last statement is, my parents were so faithful and supportive. They extended themselves beyond their means to make sure I had lessons throughout my school years and sacrificed financially to buy me a fine instrument. My parents made numerous trips to town for band and athletic activities.

As I was finishing high school I was torn between a coaching career and the music profession. I felt strongly that if I went into coaching I needed to play college football. That would not be possible, since my size and weight would not allow me to compete with the players at the university I attended, as they had an outstanding football program with many gifted athletes possessing speed, agility, size, and skill that I did not have.

I knew I could play the horn and had the potential for being successful in music. My parents were very much in favor of this decision as my mother, a former teacher, felt I could do well in the teaching profession. Each of my parents, in their own manner and focus, were a major influence and made a lasting impact on my life.

I loved the whole experience of band, practicing and spending time with my friends who were also in band and knowing I was improving very quickly. Without the extra effort of Mr. Zimmerman to search me out, I am not sure what I would have done with my life.

Our junior and senior high school band was outstanding. We won every contest we entered, playing excellent literature. In addition to the work Mr. Zimmerman did in the band area, he also directed all of the high school choral activities. If this were not enough, he determined the school needed an orchestra so he started a string program. During his fifth year in the school our full symphony orchestra of about seventy-five was invited to perform at the MENC National Convention in St. Louis. What an accomplishment. Many students from that high school program went into music in some fashion.

Mr. Zimmerman left after that year. Charles Knapp took over the program during my senior year. He was young, enthusiastic, knowledgeable, and a further inspiration to my music career. When I was about to graduate and very undecided about what I was going to do, he alone encouraged me to pursue a music education degree. I was torn at the time between music and sports, as I had an excellent football experience in high school and my coach thought I should be a coach. However, I felt that in the long run, I would much rather spend time with the kind of young people I had come to know through my many musical experiences. It proved to be a wise decision.

The next person who greatly influenced my career was my undergraduate school band director, Dr. Forrest Suycott. Not only was he an outstanding musician and teacher, but a person who was devoted to performing only the best literature of the time for band. He was also a composer and was the person who directed me toward discovering the intricacies and joy of modern music.

It was in my undergraduate years that I knew I wanted to teach, conduct, play and compose. A graduate of the University of Iowa, Dr. Syucott took me to a concert by the University of Iowa Symphony Band conducted by Frederick C. Ebbs. I thought the band at Western Illinois was a fine ensemble, which it was, but the Iowa band literally left me speechless. I had never heard a sound like that, nor enjoyed such precision and musical finesse. Following the concert I had an opportunity to meet Mr. Ebbs and found him to be very personable and open. I pretty much decided then, given the opportunity, I would do graduate work at Iowa and play in that band if at all possible.

I was accepted to Iowa as a composition major, as that had become such a passion for me. The only problem was, I still loved to play, so during that first semester I played in the marching band, symphony band, symphony orchestra, brass choir, the faculty brass quintet, and was taking trombone lessons from William Gower. Additionally, I was trying to compose the required measures each week for my composition teacher and keep up with not-so-easy graduate courses. I came close to dropping out of school from the stress of trying to do so much.

It was finally professor Gower who sat me down for a heart-to-heart and asked, "What do you really want to do when you finish?" I told him I wanted to be a high school band director and that eventually my dream was to direct and teach at the college level. I dropped composition and continued my association with Mr. Ebbs in every way possible. I learned so much from his work with the band and with the kind of rapport he developed with his students. He was a master teacher and rehearsal technician. He knew just how to achieve the sound, timbre, balance, and blend to produce a great-sounding ensemble. His personal life and the way he treated people was a constant source of guidance and inspiration. He was a champion for both standard and new literature for band, and that was reflected in his excellent programming decisions.

Little did I know that a few years later he would be my colleague at Indiana University and continue to be my mentor and source of musical inspiration until his death in 1984. Without his mentoring, lessons on organizational skills, and building outstanding bands, my tenure as the

Indiana University Director of Bands might not have been as successful as it was. Frederick Ebbs was a man of principle, spiritually devout, loyal to all in his life, and a tireless leader and magnificent musician. I will forever be indebted to him for helping me see the future and believe in my dreams.

Were there any conductors who made a lasting impression on you during your early years?

In the previous question I wrote about conductors who helped me focus and guided me into my desire to teach and conduct. In my early years of teaching in Iowa, Frederick Ebbs still was a major influence as I taught in Iowa public schools for five years following my master's degree. Since my first teaching job in Iowa was only fifteen miles from Iowa City, I would invite Professor Ebbs to visit the school and work with my band. It was during these rehearsals that my education was extended beyond the classroom. Watching Fred spin his expertise with my young musicians helped me understand the necessity of nurturing and building confidence in young, inexperienced players.

When I was a junior in college, I began making the trip to Chicago each December to attend the Midwest Clinic. This experience opened my eyes to what musical goals were possible to attain with young musicians. To observe live the unbelievable concerts by the Joliet Grade School Band under the direction of Charles Peters was truly remarkable. Watching Harry Begian conduct the Cass Technical High School Band in concerts that left the audience spellbound profoundly impacted my educational vision. Combine those concert experiences with attending clinics by teachers and conductors I had only heard about also contributed to my expectations for the profession in which I was headed.

Frederick Fennell was another figure that had emerged

in recent years. I had already heard early recordings of the Eastman Wind Ensemble, but to attend clinic presentations by this energetic and inspiring personality continued to build excitement for my chosen career.

To hear the story of how John Paynter went directly from being a graduate assistant at Northwestern to being named the Director of Bands there at such an early age was to me an incredible milestone. Even before finishing my undergraduate degree, one of my goals was to be teaching at the college or university level like John Paynter did when he was twenty-eight. Little did I know that eight years later I would be named the Assistant Director of Bands at Indiana University at the age of twenty-eight. But that is a later story and chapter in my career.

Attending the Midwest Clinic had a major impact on my career from my first years as an attendee to the present day as I am continually amazed at how this event impacts the lives of educators from all over the world.

I recall hearing a performance by the Parma Senior High School Band in 1966. Not only was the performance outstanding but also included on the program was the first high school performance of *Emblems* by Aaron Copland. The conductor of this outstanding ensemble happened to be a young woman by the name of Barbara Rankin who equally impressed me. Little did I know that two years later, I would follow Ms. Rankin at Parma Senior High School.

She had built a great program at a small school in Garner, Iowa, earning top ratings in every concert festival they entered. When she was hired at Parma Senior, most of the directors in the region gave the music supervisor a very hard time for hiring a woman for this important position. Within a few short years, this program was the finest in the state of

Ohio as well as the region.

Ms. Rankin was an inspiration to me. She accomplished so much, not because of her gender, but because she was a motivational teacher, compassionate human being, dedicated to her mission, and a consummate musician. From my perspective, she was one of the great teacher/conductors in the mid-twentieth-century band profession. It was both an honor and frightening to be her successor at Parma Senior High School.

If you could begin your college years all over again, would you do anything differently?

Given the opportunity to start my college career again, there are things I would change. Solid training with serious piano lessons would have helped me considerably, not only in my college years, but would have been a major help throughout my career, especially in score study. It was also a hindrance when I began my graduate studies in composition. All of the other composition majors were very competent on the piano, giving them a tremendous advantage while composing at the keyboard, which our teacher advocated.

I also had no theory training of any kind prior to entering college. While these elements in my music training were lacking, they were not insurmountable. I worked extra hard in those areas during my undergraduate training. I had an excellent piano teacher who gave me private lessons every week. My theory teacher was traditionally old school, but I received outstanding instruction in theory and ear training. I also found how exciting was the importance of understanding compositional elements.

When I was in high school, I am sorry to say, academic achievement was not a high priority with me. I was not a poor student by any means and was accepted to both Western Illinois

University and the University of Illinois, but I was a classic case of being an underachiever. If I had a chance to go back and change my study habits and to recognize the importance of academic achievement, my early years in undergraduate training would have been approached much differently.

Part of that realization was truly learning how to study. It was not until my junior year that I began to fully apply myself to diligent study and to focus on the importance of solid academic foundations. Knowing what I know today, I would have worked with more focus and higher academic goals prior to entering my collegiate years.

What advice can you offer to current music majors or young band directors?

My general advice to music majors preparing for a career in teaching and conducting is to be a huge musical sponge and absorb everything possible related to the profession. Keep your eyes and ears open to every aspect of your chosen field. Do not neglect practicing and performing on your major instrument to achieve the highest level of tonal, technical, and musical expression attainable. Having lofty goals in these areas will only strengthen your resolve to help your students attain similar goals.

So much can be learned through observation, processing what works and what does not work in a multitude of situations. Identify mentors whom you respect, admire, and can trust for honest evaluation and input. Listen to all forms of music. If you confine your listening to a specific area, you only limit your full understanding of musical nuance and expression.

Young band directors tend to focus so intently on the program to which they have been assigned, they forget to continue expanding their own learning curve. Attend clinics and workshops that will provide stimulation and knowledge for professional growth. For me, the Midwest Clinic provided a yearly source that allowed me to learn through clinic presentations by respected teachers and to hear ensembles that kept me focused on what was musically possible by young musicians. Conducting workshops are numerous and not expensive to attend. They provide additional opportunities to hone conducting and rehearsal skills necessary for continued growth in our art.

What were your early years of teaching like? What memories or lessons learned can you share?

My teaching experience began in Bardolph, Illinois. This was a very small rural school corporation (only fifty-two students in the entire high school) that was intent on keeping the doors open as long as possible. It is located a few miles east of Macomb, Illinois, where I attended Western Illinois University. Each year Bardolph hired a senior music education student to lead their very small instrumental music program. A new director was hired every year.

The current director typically recommended a good friend who was a junior to the school superintendent, who, in turn, hired the friend strictly on the recommendation of the current director. Each person took the Illinois test for a provisional teaching certificate so the school could legally hire a director.

I was the designated director for this one-year position. In order for me to complete my degree and do this job, which required teaching elementary through high school students, it was necessary for me to attend summer school and finish as many required courses as possible to have adequate time to fulfill my teaching responsibilities. This year proved to be so important, as it helped me establish priorities, rehearsal style, realistic goals, and how to bond with students, faculty, and parents.

Granted, the goals were not exceedingly high, given I only had seventeen students in my high school band, which included no clarinets and five drummers. (Yes drummers, not percussionists.) I did what I told my music education students at Indiana: accept the students where they are, do not blame them, and teach them to become better musicians and people.

After finishing my master's degree at the University of Iowa I taught in West Liberty, Iowa. This was another rural school district that had a fine tradition of music in the schools. My rather small band did very well as the musicians were eager, diligent in their practicing, and wanted to achieve. This is always a winning combination.

From there I took a job in Harlan, Iowa at a much larger school. In the three years I was there the program grew, requiring the school to hire an elementary/junior high director. We had a wonderful working relationship, and when I left two years later he became the head director and stayed for the next thirty-five years, continuing a fine tradition of outstanding instrumental ensembles.

During these early years of teaching, I worked very hard to maintain a truly balanced program. The hub of the program was always the concert band. All other aspects of the program stemmed from the concert band: marching band, jazz band, and solo and ensemble participation.

I firmly believe that one of the ingredients that helped these smaller programs to be successful was the focus on small ensembles. I required every member of the band to be in a small ensemble. I worked out a schedule that allowed me to hear every ensemble at least every two weeks during the entire year. This kept them accountable for their own practice schedule and advancement. Each ensemble had to participate in ensemble contest. While many students performed solos each year, solo participation at contest was not required. In smaller communities where there is a lack of private teachers, this was a way for me to teach many musical fundamentals to every member of the ensemble. I still firmly believe that small ensembles within a program can offer tremendous advantages in the musical growth of individuals.

My final high school job could not have been further from my experience at Bardolph. Parma Senior High School, just outside of Cleveland, was one of the great instrumental programs in the country, thanks to the outstanding work of Barbara Rankin. The school enrollment was 3,600 students in three grades. The band program had 180 instrumentalists. Approximately 130 of these students studied privately with top professionals in the Cleveland area, including several with Cleveland Symphony players.

This program forced me to again evaluate my own expectation level, as I was dealing with players more advanced and capable than I had experienced in my three previous high school jobs. However, the rehearsal skills and musical concepts I had established several years before remained the solid framework upon which I built new goals. Without these varied teaching experiences from such diverse schools, my collegiate teaching of music education students would not have had the impact it did. I have always been thankful for these early experiences.

How do you structure your rehearsals?
This is a question that could take many paragraphs to answer,

but I will be brief and to the point. The *music* must be the focal point of every rehearsal. I know there are times when it is necessary to cover drill, focus on fundamentals, and all the other basics.

Students must leave rehearsal with the feeling they did not want the session to end; that they were so energized and excited about what just happened they can't wait to get back to the next rehearsal. That is hard to do on a day-to-day basis, but in the end, this is what keeps students flocking to the door of the rehearsal room.

I attempt to be positive, engaging, animated, motivational, and hopefully make each member of the group feel that what they contribute is important, right down to the last-chair players in each section. This can be accomplished in the most simple of ways, by just catching a person's eye and giving a nod of approval.

Rehearsal pacing is of utmost importance in achieving an effective result. Know when to move on rather than beating a dead horse. When progress on a difficult passage begins to lag and show little to no progress, then you need to let it rest and encourage individual time on certain passages.

I believe my students appreciated the quick rehearsal style I employed. What helped me was to devise a schedule with allotted time for each piece or section of piece that is on the rehearsal schedule. I posted a rehearsal schedule for the week indicating the title of each piece, the day on which it would be rehearsed, and how much time would be spent on it. This also helps students to plan in advance.

It is amazing how much more efficient we become in rehearsal when we maintain a time allotment for each piece. Let's face it: our rehearsal style and effectiveness dictates the success of our performances. Careful planning and preparation by the director outside of rehearsal is the key to great rehearsals.

How do you approach score study?

Very carefully! This is not an on-the-job experience. Since I do not have great keyboard skills, actually, almost no keyboard skills, score study for me over the years has been difficult. When I look at a new score, I turn through the pages fairly quickly to get an overall feel for the piece in style, length, texture, tempi, range, rise and fall of dynamics, and climactic points. Even on a first read-through this can take place.

Then the process of determining melodic, harmonic and rhythmic elements come into play. For this I do two things: I use the piano (painstakingly slow) and I sing a lot of lines.

Next I want to determine the sense of form and begin to make decisions concerning phrasing. As I continue to look at particular passages, I make decisions concerning the need to manipulate dynamics, and determine what kinds of sounds I want to hear in certain passages. It is the conductor's responsibility to make these kinds of decisions prior to rehearsal. If I do not make these decisions, then the students will make these decisions and that does not always make for the best musical result.

I love examining scores. To discover the composer's intent, no matter how subtle, to me is one of the rewarding aspects of conducting. Sometimes we discover things that even the composer did not realize or intend. *Score study is the CSI of musical fulfillment.*

What is your concept of band sound? How do you achieve it?

In *Teaching Music through Performance in Band, Volume VI* (GIA G-7027), I wrote a rather lengthy chapter on band sound (Chapter 1, Soundings: Developing Beautiful Tone). It is a passion of mine to create sounds that reflect the composer's desire and to develop a sound palette that captures the attention of the listener. I am fully aware there are as many sound concepts as there are directors. That being said, each of us must adhere to strict demands from the podium to achieve the desired sound we wish to fabricate. If we do not, then once again the players in the ensemble will arrive at their own level of sound production and many times that does not prove to be satisfactory.

I prefer a sound that is well modulated, encompassing the full range of tonal colors, with the bass sounds of the ensemble supporting the rest of the range of high brass and woodwinds. Too often we hear just the opposite, with the high voices and percussion tending to dominate the color and balance of the full ensemble.

I achieved the sound I have in my head through the use of ensemble sensitivity at the beginning of every rehearsal. These simple, full-ensemble exercises helped players focus on the tonal fundamentals of balance and blend and the enrichment of overtones.

I recommend that the readers of this chapter read the chapter in *Teaching Music, Volume VI* as mentioned above. This will give you detailed information on my concept of sound and how I achieve those results.

Finally, too often I listen to ensembles that seem to be trying to play through the listener. I would rather have the audience feel like my ensemble is surrounding them in sound rather than trying to force them to listen.

What are your views on score marking?
The more diligently and systematically you study the score, the less marking is necessary! My preference is to do little marking. Mainly I mark the time changes in multi-meter pieces

only because in most scores you cannot read the changes from a normal distance because they are so small. I also mark any changes in dynamics I make. I indicate major cues so a player or section knows they can rely on a consistent preparation for an entrance. There are many concepts with color-coding, specific symbols and signs, every dynamic change, and many others. I feel if I really know the score, excessive marking is not needed.

How can we best advance our art?

Great art promotes itself. I believe that our profession has done a masterful job of advancing our art during the past two decades. The exposure to new literature, the availability of great recordings, and the fact that the world's great composers are supporting the wind band movement like never before in our history, all point to new vistas and opportunities for bands at every level.

Performance standards, conducting skills, and outstanding literature are at an all-time high in our profession. Our greatest challenge is to convince schools that this important aspect of a child's education cannot be dislodged from the offerings. In these hard economic times, the expanding academic require-ments placed on students must not end their opportunity to be a part of this musical environment. It has been proven over and over how important music participation is to the total building of character, a sense of belonging, and personal fulfillment.

> So long as the human spirit thrives on this planet, music in some living form will accompany and sustain it and give it expressive meaning.
> —Aaron Copland

What works did you program on your farewell concert?

I so much enjoyed my final concert at Indiana University. I wanted it to be a celebration about the students and the wonderful experiences that had transpired over my thirty-six-year tenure. I wanted to feature two former students who had played such an important part in the wind ensemble program, so I invited Susan Rider, who had played solo trumpet for me for seven years while she completed three degrees and is a member of the United States Marine Band in Washington DC. I also invited Matt Vaughn, whom I had known all through his high school years, a regular attendee of our Summer Music Camp, and played trombone every semester in the wind ensemble during his IU years. He went on to become a member of the Air Force band in Washington DC and then to the Philadelphia Orchestra.

Each played a solo with the ensemble and an encore, *Cousins,* which I had arranged years earlier. I also wanted to play some of my favorite music. I opened the concert with Grainger's *The Duke of Marlborough Fanfare,* and followed that with his *Lincolnshire Posy.*

There were two world premiers on the concert: *Maestro!* by Roger Clichy, which was commissioned by my department colleagues and band alumni, and *Fanfares on Re for Ray* by David Dzubay, commissioned by my wife and children. Dzubay is now head of the IU Composition Department and former trumpet player in my ensembles. These are both wonderful pieces that have had many performances since their premiers at that concert.

I also wanted to include a work that my wife and I commissioned to honor our parents. This work, *Be Thou My Vision* by David Gillingham, I am happy to say, has had hundreds of performances around the world. I concluded the program with my arrangement of *Dance of the Jester,* and of course *The Stars and Stripes Forever.*

The next day we had an Alumni Wind Ensemble concert that included a couple of works from my first concert performance at Indiana in 1969. There were also two people in the alumni band who were players in that first concert in 1969 plus some 120 other players who made up that wind ensemble. That concert was followed by a banquet that concluded the weekend events. It was a remarkable weekend, and one I will not ever forget. The students that were part of my programs were just outstanding not only in talent but even more importantly, in their character and integrity. I will forever be eternally grateful for what they brought to my life.

What are your current sources of inspiration or spiritual enrichment?

I have to first credit the Lord for His guidance, instruction, and sense of purpose in my life. My wife Molly deserves so much credit, for she has been a constant source of encouragement, support, kindness, and devoted love for the past forty-five years. The Lord has greatly blessed our life together, my career, and our life-long friendship. We are proud of our children, who are successful in their chosen fields and have provided us with six adorable grandchildren. If we would have known grandchildren were going to be so much fun, we would have had them first!

What are your interests beyond music?

Molly and I have always been outdoor people. Camping, hiking, fishing, mountain climbing, biking, skiing, and almost anything else that happens outdoors are our favorite activities. When our children were fairly young we took them camping, first close to home and then eventually to the Rocky Mountains. We all fell in love with the mountains and what they offered in the way of outdoor recreation. That is what prompted our children to work in Colorado following graduation from college. And, we knew full well after my retirement we would also live in Colorado.

Several years ago we began climbing 14,000-foot peaks in Colorado. There are fifty-three of them in the state, and we have done almost half. Living here now for three years we have grown to love the climate, the opportunity to see Pikes Peak every morning from our house, and to bask in the ever-changing colors each morning. It has also allowed me to get to know a whole new set of young directors.

To what do you attribute your exceptional musical success?

This question can probably be answered by reading responses to earlier questions. I have been blessed in so many ways, but the bottom line is, I had wonderful teachers in my early years of musical development, teachers who were inspirational, caring, visionary, creative, and willing to give of themselves to benefit their students musically and personally. I learned from my parents the need to listen to other people first, respect them, and glean life lessons that would help me mold my own philosophies and character.

The success of any teacher of any subject must be guided by an ability to communicate effectively with students in their field of expertise. None of us can or will be successful without the tools to motivate our students to reach for higher goals and not settle for mediocrity. As I tell students often, "Don't let *good* get in the way of *great*!"

Any final thoughts or words of advice?

Molly and I do a clinic titled "Making a Difference with Your Dash," in which we discuss the ability to balance personal life and professional life. It is not easy, especially these days in which life in general is threatened. I believe in teaching the importance of the difference we can make in young people's lives. I love these words of Henry Brooks Adams: "A Teacher affects eternity; they can never tell where their influence stops."

Teaching is a noble profession, and one that needs to be protected and sustained to insure the positive, forward progress of our nation and world. If I were to write my own epitaph, it would say something about my devotion to God, family, students, and profession, and that I represented music with enthusiasm, integrity, honesty, and depth of character.

I conclude this brief summary of my career with two additional quotes that I believe represent my attitude, desire, and foundation for a successful teaching career.

> You cannot be really first rate at your work, if your work is all you are.
> —Anna Quindlen in *A Short Guide to a Happy Life*

> It is the supreme art of the teacher to awaken joy in creative expression and knowledge.
> —Albert Einstein

I hope in some small way I have been able to make a difference in the lives of young musicians and helped them to discover their potential not only through music but also in building personal respect and character.

Chapter 5

JAMES CROFT

How did you begin your musical journey? Who were your first teachers and sources of inspiration?

I was to a band room born. My dad was a village and school band director with no formal training in music. He was a social science/industrial arts major who loved bands and whose first teaching job in Ringsted, Iowa in 1927 was obtained primarily on the basis of a recommendation from the bandmaster at the Iowa State Teachers College that read: "Mr. Croft plays the clarinet. He plays it very good." Now, if you were the superintendent and had a candidate with that kind of endorsement, would you look any further?

Dad, like many others of that period, attended camps and learned from those who were willing to share their expertise with someone genuinely interested in learning. Among these was Carleton Stewart, whose Mason City High School Band was one of the nation's models. Dad was a bright and naturally musical guy who did pretty well, considering his background. He eventually took his Forest City Band to the 1941 National Contest in St. Paul, Minnesota, a band in which I played third cornet!

Not playing an instrument was never an option in our family. My sisters played clarinet and horn. Dad was my first and only cornet teacher until I started taking lessons at Cornell College with Dillon Holcomb, Paula Holcomb's dad! Hugh Croft was not a particularly sensitive musician, but he was a graceful and clear conductor, and a disciplinarian. Most of his band kids called him Pop, which I think reflected well upon their affection and appreciation and spoke of their willingness to toe the mark when he marked it. He got out of the band business in 1942, realizing that he simply was not sufficiently prepared to deal with the challenges the future promised. He became involved with the Farm Bureau, and eventually did very well as a county insurance agent.

John Duckwall came to Mount Vernon High School in 1946. I had been playing in the El Kahir Shrine Band in Cedar Rapids, the college band, and with any group that paid. However, I would not play with the little kids who made up a very inexperienced school band. I was more interested in developing my modest athletic interests, basketball in particular. John struck a deal to give me conducting lessons if I played in the band. I played baritone (to learn bass clef), and John became a friend and mentor until his death. He was a pedagogue extraordinaire whose Washington High School Orchestra in Cedar Rapids was something to behold.

I did not start at Cornell College as a music major. I was

what might be called an indifferent student, not ready for the academic rigor of college. Between my freshman and sophomore years I fell from a scaffold while working on a roofing crew and suffered a broken neck, broken back, and a severe concussion. My high school coach, Walt Koch (whose sons were close friends of mine), gave me the best advice possible when he said, "What you're really good at is music. Why don't you talk to Lloyd Oakland?"

Lloyd Oakland was the director of the conservatory at Cornell, and the first thing he said to me was, "I wondered how long it was going to take you to show up!"

That three-story fall was serendipitous, for Oakland became my mentor and model. He had developed outstanding school ensembles in Indiana and Montana and brought those practical experiences to his classes where he challenged, nurtured, and demonstrated for his students. He was a gifted conductor and an outstanding musician.

Four other men were great influences on me, and each was quite unique. Fred Schroeder, band director at Lawrence University, introduced me to live performances of significant wind literature. This opened a new world of sonic design and interpretation.

Dr. Myron Russell, department chair at Iowa State Teacher's College, introduced me to effective woodwind teaching techniques, especially double reeds and reed making.
John Barrows, horn professor at The University of Wisconsin and acknowledged by many as the horn player's horn player, led me to performance practices as a hornist that were encouraging, insightful, inspiring, and extremely perceptive.

My major professor at The University of Oklahoma (and later my dean at Florida State), Dr. Robert Glidden, was and is the most natural leader I have ever known. He is extremely bright, a superb listener, a decision-maker blessed with an ingratiating personality, and a fair, caring, and visionary administrator. He was truly the ever-present guide that every doctoral student needs and every university director of bands feels blessed to have!

Were there any conductors who made a lasting impression on you during your early years?

I played for some excellent conductors, including Richard Morse and Karl Holvik, but the conductors who rang my bell were those who stood in front of the Chicago Symphony when that orchestra annually visited the Cornell College campus. For the most part, those who followed Frederick Stock were men not destined to have careers of lasting influence, but to this neophyte's ears and eyes they were almost as good as Mr. Oakland, and that was high praise indeed!

I was several years older and much, much wiser before I began to discern what conductors did musically that affected me with an intensity that was unrelenting. About this time I became aware of the efficiency and effect of Reiner, the grace of Ozawa, the dimension of Kleiber's imagination, and the excitement generated by Solti. This quartet omits, of course, dozens of others heard on recordings or in live performance. I loved watching Harry Begian, Arnald Gabriel, Don Mcginnis, Bill Revelli, Jim Neilsen, and other icons of that era work their individual magic with whatever band they led. Later, my contemporaries Bob Reynolds, John Paynter, Don Hunsberger, Frank Battisti, and a host of others provided ideas and models that were absorbed by example.

I would be remiss if I didn't mention the unique contributions made to whatever success I've known if I didn't recognize the importance of Fred Fennell, Tim Reynish, Jack Jarrett,

Gunther Schuller, and Bobby Adams, whose friendship and kinship were important when candor was critical.

If you could begin your college years all over again, would you do anything differently?

I would change but one thing if I could have it to do again: I would have seriously studied piano. My limited keyboard skills have been an impediment to efficiency and effect. I took my first piano lesson as a sophomore music major, and started practicing intensely the summer before my junior year! (Had to pass those proficiencies to graduate!) I did a few things in school I was supposed to do and a number that I shouldn't have done, and in sum, I would trade very few of them for other adventures. They add up to a collection of experiences that may have helped me recognize and reach kids who (as did I) needed a little more time and direction to find their way.

What advice can you offer to current music majors or young band directors?

To those beginning the journey of preparation, my advice is brief and succinct. Take advantage of every opportunity to hear performances rich in variety and depth. There is a reason for the admonition: *When all else fails, practice!* Your development as a performer to the point that you are an expressively responsive player has much to do with your development as a teacher of music. Be prepared to be a model.

For those entering the profession, let me suggest a few general observations honed from a lifetime of experience:

1. Listen to your elders who have been singularly successful. They have paid dues.
2. Avoid bitching and bitchers. Both are non-productive.
3. Read! Read! Read! Read widely, wisely, and well. It

is the essential mark of the character of the educator. Stay abreast of the performing arts and the humanities. You're in it!

4. Remember what your mama told you: "You're known by the company you keep." There are good guys and some not so good in every profession. Fortunately, ours is loaded with a whole bunch of good folks. Stick with 'em for life.

5. Recognize your predecessor's strengths and avoid criticism of what might appear to be their shortcomings. You gain nothing by carping on about that of which you know little or nothing. Take the opportunity to praise their accomplishments. It will bolster your image as a thoughtful colleague.

6. You get support when you give it. While we see ourselves as devoted, there will be others who see this devotion as inflexible.

7. Start and stop rehearsals on time.

8. Don't ever let your role as educator be compromised by mass entertainment.

9. Finally, we all make mistakes that we rue. Don't hesitate to say you're sorry; try not to do it again, and get over it. Tomorrow is a new day!

What were your early years of teaching like? What memories or lessons learned can you share?

I suspect all the contributors to this volume could write a book on this topic, for the subject would be so rich in personal detail that one recollection would simply prompt another. It surely has for me.

My first job was in Traer, Iowa, a typical rural cross-section of about 1,700. There were 120 in the high school and thirty-one (grades 5–12) in the band. All but a few were as green as I. It was a situation where an anxious, unsure, and apprehensive neophyte could (and did) suffer lots of mistakes, glory in a few successes, and grow like a famished flower fertilized!

How could I forget Janet Risvold auditioning for me with a memorized Rose study? I'd never heard of the Rose studies. How could I forget Earl Dunn (yes, The Earl Dunn) judiciously correcting my inept embouchure instruction while observing a clarinet lesson? He was so helpful that year. How could I forget the thrill of that unexpected State Festival Division I, the first in the school's history? It was an important affirmation, even if by the narrowest of margins.

How could I forget the embarrassment of leaving cash and checks on my desk when dashing off to a marching rehearsal, returning to find it gone, and sheepishly reporting the missing funds to my superintendent who, after letting me sweat it out a bit, opened the safe and returned the money he had discovered.

What better lesson to learn than how to deal with a colleague who disliked me before I arrived since I was to replace her closest friend? After killing her with kindness, she later became a dear friend. Good advice, that!

How grateful I was to the school janitor whose smoker's breath prompted me to quit smoking for fear that those little fourth and fifth graders would have to endure the same from me!

Finally, my favorite! After replacing twirler's problems with flags that provided an impressive five-flag front spelling TRAER, I decided at the last moment to march them down the field, do a circular countermarch, and move to the fifty-yard line for *The Star-spangled Banner.* You guessed it! They stood in all their splendor, flags boldly spelling REART!

Another lesson learned about preparation and the perils of winging it.

Those three early years provided me with a foundation that was the only grounding I needed to meet the challenges of each successive position I've held. By forgiving mistakes and encouraging success, those parents, colleagues, kids, and community were the best. I wouldn't trade one of them for anything.

How do you structure your rehearsals?

The structure of my rehearsals is probably best underscored by the old phrase, the best laid plans.... I always have the best intentions and certainly block out time allotments and objectives, but attribute the problem of suspect planning to discovery: discovering in practice that which I didn't observe in preparation. If I didn't note that many of my colleagues suffer from the same problem of time management, I'd be more concerned.

I have never spent large blocks of time tuning, even with the youngest of my ensembles. More time was spent on developing concepts of characteristic sound in my school bands which, once achieved, enabled pitch adjustments fundamental to in-tune-ness...or as I first heard from Eugene Corporon, in-tone-ness. Intonation in more mature groups is so closely related to balance and ensemble blend that it is a totally different issue. Experienced performers simply have to use the appendages on the sides of their head and adjust to the moment. I've noticed that all conductors' batons are in tune!

Every rehearsal must have variety, challenge, and that moment of satisfaction that provides performers with a sense that this has been a worthy use of time and effort. This is the same affect that keeps those of us who have had long careers recalling past moments with such pleasure.

I wish I had been a better manager of time, for my rehearsals all too often ran over their allotted span. I resented colleagues holding students over their prescribed lesson times, thus causing them to arrive late to my rehearsals. I let them know it was an imposition on the rest of my ensemble. I can only beg forgiveness when committing the same transgression. May the reader beware.

Little is accomplished by those extra minutes, for concentration ebbs near the wee-bitching hour.

How do you approach score study?

I am an avid and fairly rapid reader of words, and a laboriously slow reader of scores. Over the years, as a result of hours and hours of study, I've gotten better; not good, but better. I was always coached by Lloyd Oakland to sing parts and found the early LeBlanc publications by Karl Holvik and Jim Neilsen to be especially helpful. I later used the suggestions found in both the Ernst-Hunsberger and the Battisti-Garofolo conducting texts to be supportive.

Audiating what I thought I heard and then checking it, note by note and line by line became my study mantra. You can see why it took me so long to work out complex scores! If I had access to a good, or even adequate recording it would save tons of time, but it is also very easy to start relying on the recording and ignoring what is on the page.

There is no substitute for systematic score study. Find a system that best fits your skills and hone them, focusing on what is effective in the rehearsal. There is something to the admonition that the proof of the pudding is… Experience may not be the most efficient teacher, but it surely helps.

I add in passing that I love the challenge of a good crossword puzzle. It requires a reasonable vocabulary, a familiarity with historical moments of importance, a level of comfort with current events, and a general knowledge of the world about us. As the words and letters coalesce to complete the puzzle, it is not at all unlike the study of a good score. Once completed, you are ready to rehearse!

What is your concept of band sound? How do you achieve it?

My thoughts on band sound have changed over the years. Some of this is due to hearing different models, some the result of hearing professionals, some the product of music new to me, and much of it due to the resources I had at hand.

I was overwhelmed with the sound of the St. Olaf College Choir the first time I heard them with Melius Christianson and later with his son at the helm, and even now with Anton Armstrong leading this remarkable group. I had the same experience when Weston Nobles' Luther College Nordic Choir touched me profoundly, as it has ever since. The work of Robert Shaw opened my ears to another choral sensation, as did the work of my long-time colleagues at Oshkosh High School, Fred Leist and Larry Klaus. I mention each of these for they were all different. All reflected personalities, preferences of sound, and interpretations that were true to their preferences. There was no correct or incorrect. They were all superb.

With this as a prelude, let me say that I thought my dad's band had a great sound. It was the only sound I knew until I heard Careton Stewart's Mason City Band. Whoa! New day! They were wonderful, and remained my idea of ideal until I heard Frank Piersol's bands. His Iowa State and Iowa University Bands opened my ears to a more mature dimension.

However, nothing moved me like the first hearing of William D. Revelli's University of Michigan Symphonic Band.

The bar had been lifted, and the warmth, richness, and depth of that sonority was forever tattooed on my mind as the ideal sound of a symphonic band.

Then came an epiphany! Frederick Fennell brought his Eastman Wind Ensemble to Chicago's Orchestra Hall, and my sound world changed. Soon after that, I heard the International Staff Band of the Salvation Army, quite another combination of wind-driven sounds. Finally, the impact of the Netherlands Wind Ensemble was such a sensitizing experience that I was delirious with pride to be a part of this profession of wind conductors responding to an ever-expanding literature that required attention, not to *a* sound, but to the infinite variety of sounds that was available to me. That is my ideal sound!

What are your views on score marking?
I used to mark my scores profusely, going through a period of marking all cues, dynamics, and structure with various coded colors. The end result was a pretty page, but a set of colors that kept the eyes on the page and the head in the score. As I moved away from this practice, I found that a soft pencil (no. 1–1/2) for cues and structure helped me keep my head out of the score and my eyes where they belonged.

Especially for major works, I do like to have a study score that I can mark up with abandon and a rehearsal score that notes only the critical concerns that might need attention. Generally, less is more!

How can we best advance our art?
Reflect, read, and listen to those of a similar persuasion; stay in touch with the wider world of art and creative spirit; and, as experience is assimilated, remember your responsibilities to those you serve: your students and your audience.

Remember where you came from, where you are, and where you're going. We have been somewhat burdened by our functional history, but only somewhat. The wind-driven medium that we know today is one that I have personally witnessed over the past sixty-plus years, and it has grown in quality and sophistication beyond the wildest of expectations. Even better, the future promises to be even richer as composers, on whose efforts we rely, explore the expressive possibilities of our medium. I wish I could be around for another sixty or so years to see and to hear what I know will be a new age for winds and those who guide it!

What works did you program on your farewell concert?
Well, there wasn't one; there were three! The April 25 concert was orchestrated by my partner and associate, Patrick Dunnigan. This included works that were commissioned for the event and were conducted by colleagues. The commissioned works included:

Kim Archer	*To Stop the Band* (a fanfare by a former student and a round I've used as a warm-up for years)
Dan Godfrey	*Colors Aloft*
Fridges Hides	*Symphonic Movement* (a dear Hungarian friend)
Frank Ticheli	Symphony no. 2, movements 1 and 2 (conducted by my good friend, Donald Hunsberger)

The Ticheli was the product of a consortium led by former student John Carmichael. A number of former students and friends joined in the commission. Nothing could have touched me more.

I conducted the April 26 concert by the Wind Orchestra. The music consisted of a variety of career and personal favorites:

Charles Belsterling	*March of the Steelmen* (first played in my Dad's National Concert Band in 1941)
Richard Wagner	*Trauersinfonie* (the signature piece of Traer High School Band's first State Festival Division I in 1952)
David Del Tredici	*In Wartime* (premiere performance sponsored by a consortium)
Percy Grainger	*Colonial Song* (a tribute to a composer important to the band world with solo parts sung by colleagues)
R. R. Bennett	*Suite of Old American Dances* (a favorite wherever I've taught)
Jules Massenet/ Daniel Harding	*Meditation from Thais* (with flute choir in and about the hall, a sound that I love)
Jack Jarrett	*Choral Symphony* (composed during Jarrett's residency as a Ford Foundation composer for the Oahkosh High School A Cappella Choir and Concert Band)

The sayonara concert was at the World Association of Symphonic Bands and Ensembles International Conference in Jonkoping, Sweden, July 1 2003, and featured music with an FSU connection: commissions, former students, colleagues, and soloists.

Donald Grantham	*Come, Memory*
Frank Ticheli	Symphony no. 2
Eric Ewazen	*Concerto for Bassoon and Winds* (Jeffrey Keesecker, bassoon)
Teilman Susato/	
Patrick Dunnigan	*Selections from the Danserye.* (Patrick Dunnigan, conductor)
David Del Tredici	*In Wartime*
Scott McAlister	*Black Dog* (Frank Kowalsky, clarinet)

What are your current sources of inspiration or spiritual enrichment?

Whatever touches my heart, causes me to question and reflect, stimulates alternative ideas, and provides insight. This is often music and literature, but not infrequently interaction with friends whose judgment or wisdom I have come to admire.

My wife of fifty-nine years has dealt with Multiple Sclerosis for over thirty years, and I have been dealing with Parkinson's disease for about a decade. (We say we are a neurologist's dream team!) Living with someone who has dealt heroically with such an insidious affliction has made it much easier to live with my own limitations. This is about as inspirational as I can imagine.

Watching your grandchildren grow into the neat kids they are is almost more enrichment than one person can handle. As Don Wilcox told me, "If I'd known how much fun grandkids are, I'd have skipped raising their parents!"

What are your interests beyond music?

Reading, listening, history, sports, travel, enjoying vicariously the success of students and friends, being a grandpa, and glorying in my good fortune of having known all of these.

To what do you attribute your exceptional musical success?

Being at the right place, with the right colleagues, with the right opportunities, at the right time; to the right parents, the right partner, and a lot of good fortune to use whatever native ability was nurtured by the right teachers, environment, and friends.

If you could do it all over again, would you do anything differently?

I don't think so. You can't count on being blessed by such good fortune a second time!

How would you like your epitaph to read?

I don't want to think about epitaphs.

Any final thoughts or words of advice?

I believe that this project, *The Conductor's Legacy,* inspired by the life and work of Frederick Fennell, has given each of the respondents an opportunity to reflect on a career that has a common thread. The *Band* has been good to each of us, and we have all, in our separate ways, been good for the *Band.* Aren't we lucky?

Chapter 6
COL. ARNALD GABRIEL

How did you begin your musical journey? Who were your first teachers and sources of inspiration?

My musical journey began when I was about seven or eight years old. My dad took me to the basement of Saint Anthony's Church in Cortland, NY to hear a touring group from Syracuse, NY perform *Cavallaria Rusticana*. The sets were very meager and the orchestra consisted of a piano, a few strings, and a couple of winds. But when they played the *Intermezzo Sinfonica*, I was absolutely taken with its passion and beauty. To this day, I think it is the most beautiful forty-eight measures of music ever written.

When I was ten or eleven, I took my first lesson on flute, and played in both the junior high school band and orchestra.

The first teacher who provided musical inspiration was Burton Stanley. It is important at this point to stress the impact he had on my life. I graduated from Cortland High School in June 1943 and enlisted in the Army one week later. After having served as a combat machine gunner in the famed 29th Infantry Division for 201 days on the front line, fighting from Normandy to the Elbe River, I was a confused and troubled young man.

> [The 29th Infantry was depicted in the movie, *Saving Private Ryan*. Col. Gabriel is too modest to mention that he was highly decorated for bravery in action. He was awarded two Bronze Stars, the Combat Infantryman's Badge and the French Croix de Guerre—Ed.]

Upon returning to Cortland, I felt I was a social misfit. I took a job in a canning factory for eighty-seven cents an hour! During the summer of 1946, professor Stanley came to the factory and asked what I was doing there. I replied that I was earning a living. He asked why I had not applied to go to college. I felt that there was no way that I could compete with high school students who were practiced musicians, and with GIs who had played in military bands. I had not played an instrument in three years.

Professor Stanley went to his alma mater, Ithaca College, registered for me, paid my matriculation fee, waived my audition, and recommended me to Walter Beeler (the band director) and Craig McHenry (the orchestra director). I made first chair in both band and orchestra, which I'm sure I did not deserve. Professor Stanley advised the faculty at Ithaca to put pressure on me. I was slated to play on the first student recital in October.

I agreed to try college for one semester. Frightened by all

of the pressure, I practiced four or five hours a day, often until midnight, so that I would not disappoint Professor Stanley. The rest, as they say, is history. I have held Professor Stanley in my prayers every day, and have funded a scholarship in his name at Ithaca College. As he approaches his ninety-fourth birthday (in 2009), I want him to know the tremendous impact that he has had on my life, and the love I have for him.

Were there any conductors who made a lasting impression on you during your early years?

It was not only Professor Stanley who made a lasting impression, but also Walter Beeler and Craig McHenry. Students who played for both of them for four years were given an invaluable education. Walter Beeler was a taskmaster who stressed rhythm, precision, balance, and blend. Craig McHenry (who was Irish) insisted on phrasing, tone quality, and a *bel canto* style, which he often demonstrated with his beautiful Irish tenor voice. By combining the attributes of both of these professional musicians, one came away with a complete ensemble education. Both of them had a professional background, having performed as soloists with the famed Patrick Conway Concert Band.

If you could begin your college years all over again, would you do anything differently?

I do not believe I would have done anything differently in college. I made it a point to play every instrument in the concert band for at least one semester in one of the repertory bands.

What advice can you offer to current music majors or young band directors?

Current music majors often ask me how to get experience in

conducting. My answer is that you have to make your own opportunities. While I was a sophomore at Ithaca I went to the mayor of Homer, NY (which is adjacent to Cortland) and asked what had happened to the library and instruments of the Homer Band (conducted by Patrick Conway before he formed his own professional band). I discovered that everything was stored in the basement of City Hall. With local players from Cortland, Homer, and Ithaca College, I re-formed the Homer Band and played summer concerts during my last three years at Ithaca. I also conducted the Memorial Baptist Choir and the Cortland Drum and Bugle Corps.

What were your early years of teaching like? What memories or lessons learned can you share?

My early years of teaching are somewhat different from those graduates who teach in the public schools. In 1951 we were immersed in the Korean conflict and I had no desire to go back into the infantry. I enlisted in the Air Force as a band director for the duration of the Korean conflict. I liked what I was doing, so I decided to make it a career. My first assignment was at Sampson Air Force Base near Geneva, NY, an induction center. I was able to recruit many college graduates, including some from Fred Fennell's Wind Ensemble and some undergraduate students from Ithaca College.

I must confess that I probably learned more than I taught during the period between 1951 and 1955 just through listening to those advanced players. Few people have had the opportunity to work with players of that caliber during their first years of teaching and conducting.

How do you structure your rehearsals?

The structure and anatomy of my rehearsals depends on the

group being rehearsed. If it is a professional group and you are on the clock, you step on the podium and begin with the first piece scheduled for rehearsal. Professional groups do not want to be lectured.

With student groups, I always start by tuning. I try to plan my rehearsal time with a definite structure in mind. Everything must be accomplished in the time allocated.

An aside is probably appropriate here. As a guest conductor, one must be business-like but not abrasive. On the other hand, being a cheerleader (telling a group they are terrific when they are not just to win their approval) is insulting and counterproductive.

How do you approach score study?

I approach a score by looking for the overall structure first in order to determine form, high points, places of repose, areas that may pose performance problems, etc. I try to internalize the score the way an architect looks at a blueprint: to conceive it as a whole.

What is your concept of band sound? How do you achieve it?

The concept of the band sound depends on the composer's intent. One of the most difficult considerations is dealing with dynamics. A composer never knows how many instruments will play a figure, melody, or accompaniment. I have conducted groups from forty-five to 145. So what constitutes *forte* for a passage? The conductor must adjust dynamics constantly to achieve proper balance. How to achieve a band sound is quite complex and differs from band to band. As we used to say in the infantry: "It depends upon the terrain."

What are your views on score marking?

I mark the score very little. I have seen conductor's scores marked so drastically as to render the notes illegible. Put the markings in your head!

How can we best advance our art?

We can advance our art by challenging our musicians, performing a well-balanced program for our audiences, commissioning new works, and continuing to fight for a reasonable budget for our program, whether it be in an academic, military, community, or other venue.

What works did you program on your farewell concert?

The final Air Force Band concert included:

Giuseppe Verdi/Lake	*La forza del destino*
Carmen Dragon	*I Am An American* (Lynda Day George, narrator)
Jerry Bilk	*Preludium and March* (the premiere performance, dedicated to the conductor)
Floyd E. Were	*Concerto for Trumpet* (Doc Severinsen, soloist)
P. I. Tchaikovsky/Lake	*1812 Overture* (William Conrad, conductor)
Floyd E. Were	*The Story of the Battle Hymn of the Republic* (Peter Graves, narrator)

This was not my *final* concert. In addition to an active conducting schedule, I have a contract to conduct the Wheaton, Illinois Municipal Band when I am 100 years old... and *that* will not be my final concert!

What are your current sources of inspiration or spiritual enrichment?

My source of inspiration is my faith. I am not a particularly religious person, but I am very spiritual. I also am reminded of a common phrase heard often during my war days: "There are no atheists in the foxhole."

I draw a great deal of inspiration from friends. The love of family and friends runs very deeply, and their spirit manifests itself on the podium.

What are your interests beyond music?

Other interests include more music, family, and friends, and when I am well, golf.

To what do you attribute your exceptional musical success?

I am still trying to achieve it. My dad told me just before I took my first lesson that when Giuseppe Verdi lay dying, he said, "I have but one regret having to die at this time. I was just beginning to learn something about music." I have never forgotten that. It is truly the journey, not the destination.

How would you like your epitaph to read?

I will leave my epitaph to others. I have no idea what I would say.

Any final thoughts or words of advice?

I think I have covered my philosophy fairly thoroughly. Throughout history, a musical career has never been easy, but it is truly the most spiritual and passionate pursuit of man. Having performed in all fifty of the United States and fifty-nine countries of the world, I have witnessed the impact music has. I have seen Americans weep in Moscow upon hearing our national anthem; Communists cheering for American music, Muslims praising an American band, Buddhists smiling (however reluctantly), the Mormon Tabernacle Choir rejoicing unabashedly, and Pope John XXIII asking to pose for a photo with the band after we had played for 70,000 in Saint Peter's Square. The examples are endless.

To be a musician is a blessing from God.

Chapter 7

H. ROBERT REYNOLDS

How did you begin your musical journey? Who were your first teachers and sources of inspiration?

I received an E-flat alto horn for Christmas when I was in the fourth grade. I was terribly disappointed, but I put on a good face so my mother and grandparents would not think I was ungrateful. My first lessons were from my Grandfather, a self-taught band director (there's a really terrific story there also). A few years later I switched to French horn.

Were there any conductors who made a lasting impression on you during your early years?

I had the opportunity to be at a concert conducted by Arturo Toscanini, but I was too young (probably early high school) to really appreciate his talent and inspiration. My high school band director helped me greatly, first as my private teacher, then as a student conductor of my high school band where he offered many helpful suggestions. Thanks to my high school band director, Paul Inglefield, I already had a great deal of experience and skill when I took beginning conducting in college.

If you could begin your college years all over again, would you do anything differently?

No. I think it is important to go to the very best school you can *regardless of cost.* Become the finest musician you can, and learn to play your instrument at the level of a performance major even though you are headed toward the profession of conducting in the schools. The quality of education is so important, and that is in large part a result of being in an atmosphere of high-level music making. The sounds being put into your ears from other musicians will provide a foundation for excellence.

What advice can you offer to current music majors or young band directors?

Be the best musician you can be. Don't let administrative tasks take precedence over musical preparation and development. Know the individual instruments *very, very* well.

Treat everyone with kindness and respect. What you do speaks louder than what you say.

What were your early years of teaching like? What memories or lessons learned can you share?

My first job was in a town of 600. There were 1,000 students in the school (K–12). Most of the students were bused in from farms in the area. I was also a basketball coach, and played on the town basketball team.

I taught all levels, from beginning band (fifth grade) through high school. I learned more than the students. At this point I was *very* determined (a good thing), but did not always keep my temper in check in rehearsals (a bad thing). My high school band gave me a bright red ski sweater as a Christmas present with a note inside saying, "Here's a sweater to match your temper." *Wow!* I totally reevaluated my rehearsal manner at that point.

Later, in my second position at a much larger high school, I read a great deal, searching for knowledge to help me be the best teacher and musician I could be. One of the books which had a deep impact on me was *Of Music and Music Making* by Bruno Walter. Walter indicated that the dictatorial approach (my former method) results in the players' resistance or intimidation, and that neither results in the ideal atmosphere which I was and still am trying to achieve.

How do you structure your rehearsals?

At the beginning, along with tuning there is usually music that promotes sensitive listening. This is the most essential ingredient. I also believe that the tuning process is overvalued. The most effective tuning takes place during the course of rehearsal.

Next is the music in which the greatest amount of intensive work must take place. I firmly believe that conductors should internalize the sound of the composition so that differences can be heard and altered to meet their preconceptions.

The conclusion of the rehearsal is a time to put together those aspects that were the focus of the rehearsal and to conclude in a satisfying or pleasurable manner.

How do you approach score study?

Each score is its own challenge. There is no single way to approach a score. I always try to find out what makes this piece this piece? What is the structure? What is important? In some cases it is harmony, or thematic development, or motivic variation, etc.

I also try to reduce the composition to its most basic version, often without window dressing such as instrumentation. As I sit with a new score, I usually have a pad of paper beside me on which to make notes. In order to find those aspects I believe important, I look for differences: changes in time, instrumentation, key, volume, texture—changes, changes, changes. I then ask myself "Why is this change here?" I am looking for clues.

Composers write the notes and the marks around the notes to communicate their intentions. It is the conductor's job to take those notes (clues) and to find the composer's meaning. I am *very* interested in determining the direction of the composition both in overall architecture and also in the small phrases and moments, even isolated notes. In addition, I put a high priority on balance of individual lines and sections.

One is never finished with score study; it is a never-ending process. It is both rewarding and frustrating. It is very much like attempting to solve a mystery that can't be completely solved. A conductor must go well beyond just the road map aspects of the clarinets come in here, it is *mezzo forte*, hold the fermata, etc. There is no more important aspect for a conductor than score study; not conducting technique, not rehearsal technique...*nothing!*

What is your concept of band sound? How do you achieve it?

I believe that a band sound is a thing of the past. You cannot have a single sound that is appropriate for Mozart and Wagner, Bach and Persichetti, Stravinsky and Copland, Brahms and Sousa. Each piece has its own sound in the same way that an accent is different in the music of Haydn, Beethoven, Brahms, Stravinsky, and Messiaen. Each piece of music has its own personality, and conductors must uncover that personality. Only then will they know what sound is correct for that piece.

What are your views on score marking?

I used to mark my scores a great deal. Now there are very few marks in my scores. I found that with a heavily marked score I was only reading marks and was not aware as much of the other aspects as they were being played. I do, however, mark certain things so that I can shortcut the information my eyes take in. These include changes of time, especially if there is a great deal of mixed meter. I have developed my own shorthand for mixed meter. I also mark instrument abbreviations, especially if an instrument enters at the end of a page of a full score.

How can we best advance our art?

We advance our art by being artistic individuals ourselves. We are representatives of our art by all we do, say, and are. By performing the very finest compositions of *real* merit, and through collaborating with composers via commissions and other means we help create a community between composers and conductors... especially band conductors.

What works did you program on your farewell concert?

Richard Strauss	*Wiener Philharmoniker Fanfare*
Paul Hindemith	*Symphony in B-flat*
Leslie Bassett	*Lullaby for Kirsten*
Michael Daugherty	*Rosa Parks Boulevard* (premiere)
Percy Grainger	*Lincolnshire Posy*
William Bolcom	*Song* (premiere)
Gustav Holst	*First Suite in E-flat*
Percy Grainger	*Irish Tune from County Derry* (encore)

What are your current sources of inspiration or spiritual enrichment?

Many: God, family (especially my wife, Kristin, and my three daughters: Susie, Patti Jo, and Kirsten), many, many good and long-time friends; time to just think about love, people, the world, the art of music making, creativity, and perhaps most important, time to think of nothing at all.

What are your interests beyond music?

History. The American revolutionary period, especially Thomas Jefferson, as well as World War II, photography, table tennis, sports cars, and travel.

To what do you attribute your exceptional musical success?

Being inquisitive enough to risk embarrassment; continuing to learn even though people now think I'm an expert (little do they know!)

Growth is essential to anyone who wishes to be alive. As the saying goes, "Change is inevitable—growth is an option." I try to live a musical life and have music as a part of my daily life.

If you could do it all over again, would you do anything differently?

I would try to compose more, even if I believed that my compositions were inadequate. I gave this up before I had a chance to try and fail.

How would you like your epitaph to read?

I hope it reads, "He made a difference."

Any final thoughts or words of advice?

I believe it is past time for our profession (band and wind ensemble conducting) to make music the way the rest of the world makes music. In every performance there are really two performances: the first we do so well—that of being sure that we have eliminated the audible error (intonation, precision, correct notes, appropriate balance, proper style, etc.) What we have left on the back burner is communicating the inner essence of the meaning of the music: how it feels, the internal rush of emotion, the quiet solitude, and so many and varied emotions.

Music communicates soul to soul. It is not intended to be sanitary. The more we make music—real music, true music—the greater and more profound will be the purpose and more significant the rewards for our students and listeners. The sooner we stop seeking the fame and glory of perfection the sooner we will enjoy the ultimate rewards of our worthy quest: *music.*

[Since *The Conductor's Legacy* is dedicated to Frederick Fennell, Maestro Reynolds offered the following brief, insightful memory of a life-altering event.—Ed.]

My first meeting with Frederick Fennell

Early in my tenure at Long Beach State (I must have been thirty years old), I was selected to conduct the All-Southern California High School Honor Band. This was the very first honor band I ever conducted. Frederick Fennell conducted half the concert and I, the other half, but I was to prepare his music as well as the music I selected. Since Dr. Fennell would only be able to rehearse shortly before the concert, my preparation of his music was crucial to the success of the concert. It turned out that I prepared his music even more diligently than I did my own, for I envisioned that he would mount the podium, begin to rehearse, then say, "Everything is just the way I want it; no need for more rehearsal." You see, I had studied his recordings and knew all his little innuendos, tempos, balances, and musical nuances. Everything was perfect, and the band was performance ready.

Well, what actually happened was that he came to my "perfect" preparation and just took off musically. I had never witnessed a rehearsal like that. There was so much energy and knowledge, and such great ears. I had never seen gestures that so vividly described the music. I was blown away, and it changed my life forever.

[Maestro Reynolds asked that his oldest daughter, Susie, proof his copy for this chapter. Susie provided an insightful description of a Reynolds rehearsal given below—Ed.]

Observations of a Reynolds rehearsal

My view from the peanut gallery on how my dad rehearses is:

1. He creates an atmosphere in which each player is expected to arrive at the first rehearsal as prepared as possible.

2. He generally has the group play through the entire piece or movement during the initial rehearsal with minimal stopping to hear or assess what he's dealing with.

3. Immediately after the first run-through, he picks certain sections to work on and improve. This shows the players what he expects and how he and the group are going to achieve their goals.

4. It is common for him to sing parts or passages to demonstrate the sound that he hears internally.

    a. Sometimes I have heard him ask an entire section to sing a part aloud to hone in on a particular problem without instruments involved.

    b. He sometimes purposely singles out one or two players or sections that have nailed the idea of the piece through interpretation and/or technical virtuosity.

    c. The huge side effect of this is that other players sit up straighter in their seats and pay attention with more detail and focus. They see that you expect and reward greatness in them.

    d. The musicians understand that it's okay to explore different ways to play the same notes and that they will be rewarded by the end result of the enhanced musical experience, and/or recognition from the conductor and other players.

5. Sometimes, when group members really gel with each other and the conductor, a sense of lifting off happens. Everyone has a heightened experience and is reminded of the sweet sense of why they are musicians. It is actually a palpable feeling that some will discuss as they are leaving the rehearsal.

6. This, of course, inspires players to prepare more for

the next rehearsal with a greater sense of the musical goal and instills a sense of pride in individual and overall accomplishment. In most groups, this spreads to other players who, in kind, praise their fellow musicians during rehearsals.

7. Where possible, have composers attend and participate in a later rehearsal of their piece.

    a. This enriches the musical experience and provides first-hand feedback regarding the intent and purpose of the music. It also provides the added benefit revealing the flexibility of the piece to the players, allowing them to move with the group, composer, and conductor to allow it to take its best shape.

    b. Players also witness the conductor taking direction from the composer, and watch with a keen eye as to how the conductor translates and transforms the composer's intentions and insights into concrete changes in the conducting behavior and the musical experience. Quite fascinating to watch.

Chapter 8

RICHARD STRANGE

How did you begin your musical journey? Who were your first teachers and sources of inspiration?

In the small rural Kansas towns and country schools of the 1930s there were essentially no meaningful music classes other than group singing directed by whatever teacher could carry a tune using *The Yellow Book of Favorite Songs* or the Green *Happy Hour* as source material. Sometimes there was a piano in the school, sometimes not.

When I was very young, my grandmother (father's side) sang to me often while accompanying herself at an upright pedal organ. Mother was a good violinist, but seldom had time to play her instrument during those penurious times.

My formal music training started when we finally moved to

Hutchinson, Kansas, where I joined the beginning high school band on clarinet. I became fascinated by the instrument and by the band. By the second year I was moved progressively up to first chair in both the top band and the small orchestra. I also learned to play the alto saxophone in order to join the dance band that was being formed at the local Hutchinson Youth Center.

Were there any conductors who made a lasting impression on you during your early years?
Roland Gunn, the Hutchinson High School band and orchestra director, was the kind man and good musician who guided my high school efforts. He was a master at creating solo and ensemble activities for us in addition to the regular daily band routine. He urged me to attend the nationally known music camp held each summer at Western State College, Gunnison, Colorado, where I fell under the tutelage (and spell) of William D. Revelli, University of Michigan band director. Immediately I wanted to be a band director—a path from which I never deviated.

If you could begin your college years all over again, would you do anything differently?
A lack of family finances made it necessary for me to start my first year at Hutchinson Junior College. The lack of solid music theory classes and advanced ensembles made it obvious to me that a transfer to a four-year school was necessary, so, with money I was now earning with local dance bands and the awarding of a half-tuition scholarship ($30.00 per semester), I switched to Wichita University, a small, inexpensive municipal school at that time. Here Walter Duerksen had assembled a good music school with several outstanding teachers. James Robertson was a particularly impressive conductor of the

excellent orchestra. I copied all his conducting mannerisms verbatim and use him as one of my models to this day.

What advice can you offer to current music majors or young band directors?

1. My theory and piano skills suffered from inattention, and I have wished many times since my formal training ended that I could go back and pick up these necessary musical skills; but there has never seemed to be enough hours in the day to do so. Try to remedy your musical deficiencies as you go through your undergraduate years.

2. Choose your mentors wisely and learn to play all the instruments at a high level if you are to teach them well.

What were your early years of teaching like? What memories or lessons learned can you share?

Some truisms just may be true. My truism of the day is: "You can't teach what you don't know."

I suspect that most young band directors start their careers as I did, with knowledge varying from good to sensational concerning their own major instrument, and very little specific knowledge about most of the other instruments of the band. Those who are conscientious soon realize their dearth of practical wisdom and seek (sometimes half-heartedly) to remedy this teaching defect.

My first rehearsal connected with my first teaching job showed me in no uncertain terms that my mind was a veritable *tabula rasa* in respect to most band instruments. After futilely trying to push my young eighteen-member band through an extremely simple piece of music, I was confronted with the raised arm of a bewildered young baritone horn player. "Mr. Strange," he asked, "what is the fingering for D-flat?"

(I don't remember the actual note, but everything else is true.) Shamefaced, my reply was, "I don't know, but I'll tell you tomorrow," which I did, after struggling that evening to relate the baritone horn, which I didn't know, to the trumpet, which I did know. After all these years, I still remember this episode and its consequence vividly, which was my solemn vow to myself to learn to play all the band instruments as well as I possibly could.

My learning method was a simple one. I bought a beginning book for each of the band instruments in turn and started with page one. Not having anyone to guide me in that small town in Kansas, I floundered around a great amount, but the first thing I tried to do when practicing each instrument was to achieve a respectable quality of tone, characteristic of one produced by fine professional players. I soon learned that it was necessary to have good equipment (horn, mouthpiece, reed, etc.), and so I started purchasing each of the woodwind instruments as I had time to work on them.

All of this took an untold amount of time, but there was not much else to do in that small town, and it seemed the most productive way to spend my spare hours. It helped to live one-half block from the school, where I could always find one of the larger instruments left behind by a non-practicing student.

After the first year of this practice regimen I became confident enough of my playing prowess to use all the various instruments, one by one, as a teaching tool in my fifth-grade beginning band classes. From that point on, I taught with a different horn in my hand each class period, and soon found out that no matter how undeveloped my playing skills were they were better than those of my beginning students, partially because I could read notes and count rhythms.

Almost immediately my students, who now had a playing role-model, and not just a talking head, started to produce better sounds themselves, and were highly critical of my progress, since I had confessed to them that I was learning these instruments just as they were.

Over a period of seven years, with the help of many other teachers and players, I really did learn to play all the band instruments as well as (or better than) most of my students, both grade school and high school. Because I had experienced every conceivable beginning problem on each instrument, I found myself more and more able to recognize student problems and suggest the same remedies that had helped me to overcome the same problems. I became convinced then, and remain convinced now, that the ability to play all the band instruments well is the surest way to give yourself the tools necessary to be a fine band director.

Most college music education curricula contain more work on secondary instruments than was the case when I was in school many years ago. However, having taught many of those courses on the college level in years past, I find that most students neither progress to any lasting extent on the minor instruments nor have any real wish (or time) to do so. They put in most of their practice time on a major instrument and spend the rest in ensembles making music on a high level (one hopes). They have no current need to know the material to which they are exposed.

This readiness to learn affects students on all levels of the educational process. My need to know came during the first rehearsal of my first day's teaching. From that day on, there was no question in my mind that I needed the information I had so cavalierly rejected in my undergraduate years. Shame is a great motivator.

Here are my suggestions, *vis-à-vis* learning to play all the band instruments:

1. Take up the instruments one at a time, starting with your worst instrument. Don't consciously try to relate one instrument to another, but treat each one as if you were beginning to major on that instrument.

2. Make certain that you use good equipment. If you use a school instrument or one left in the band room by an erring student, be certain to purchase your own top-quality mouthpiece and reeds. Seek help in these matters from colleagues who are fine performers on the instrument in question. Remember, cheap equipment produces bad results for beginners of all ages, including yourself.

3. If at all possible, purchase your own instrument. I found quickly that the outlay of my own hard-earned money to purchase the best instrument I could afford was a great incentive for consistent practice.

4. As soon as possible, purchase a quantity of solo material and standard etude books to keep up your musical interest. After I rushed through a beginning book I always started working on a solo in the standard repertoire regardless of how amateurishly I was forced to play it because of lack of technical ability. For instance, shortly after I purchased a bassoon I started working on the Mozart *Bassoon Concerto* simply because I loved the music. I was not able to publicly perform it satisfactorily for several years, but I enjoyed noodling through various passages almost from the beginning.

5. Before you think you should, volunteer to perform on your current minor instrument in some ensemble,

church group, municipal band, dance band, etc. This can be a great inducement for concentrated practice on music that will be heard by others.

For instance, I was playing lead alto in a typical territory dance band when we suddenly lost our lead trumpet player. Since I was working hard on the trumpet I volunteered to take on the chair because a satisfactory replacement could not be found. (Another alto sax player was available). For the next five years I hung on to that chair, learning an immense amount about playing jazz trumpet. Although all of this takes *chuzpah*, it worked for me.

6. Try as hard as possible to take occasional lessons on your secondary instruments. Just be certain that your teacher sounds the way you wish to sound and makes sense to you when discussing the playing techniques of the instrument involved.

    I managed to persuade my Master's Degree Committee at the University of Colorado to include private secondary lessons with the top teachers during each of the four summers it took for me to complete my degree plan. This was some of the most valuable training that I received at that fine institution.

7. Read and compare all possible technical and pedagogical articles that you can lay your hands on. Try out all suggestions, and use those that seem to make *you* a better player. Don't be afraid to take the conflicting material in various articles with a grain of salt. Use what works for you in your own playing and reject the rest. If a suggestion does not work for you, it probably won't work for your students either.

8. Go to as many as clinics and music meetings as possible

and participate fully in the various activities and offerings. Ask questions; the only bad question is an unasked
one. I have always been an inveterate conference- and
clinic-goer, thus gathering pertinent information that I
could not seem to find in periodicals and books.

9. Be assured that the mastery of each succeeding instrument
    becomes quicker and easier than the one before. Learning
    to play all the wind instruments is one of the most musi-
    cally satisfying tasks to which we can set ourselves. It has
    been a never-ending source of pleasure to me.

All fine band directors motivate their students to practice
the basic techniques necessary to play fine repertoire. Through
many subtle and not-so-subtle means the director requests
(demands) a great amount of practice time from each student
if superior musical results are to be obtained. Can we demand
any less from ourselves? Which should be more important to
the superior educator: the ability to participate in aesthetic
music-making, utilizing all the various tools of the trade, or
a good golf score? Which is more important: the ability to
demonstrate characteristic tone quality and proper fingering
sequences on all the instruments, or knowing the continuing
plot of the latest sitcom? Your answers to questions like these,
at least in part, will determine your future worth as a teacher.
Practice takes time. You have the time. Use it.

Secondly, I started out as a band director trying to mimic
Dr. Revelli's every gesture and mannerism, but convinced
myself as soon as I started working with Hugh McMillan
at the University of Colorado that his graciousness gave the
same musical results without the fear factor. It seems obvious
to me now that a genuine desire on the part of the teacher to
impart knowledge within the range of his own personality

traits always produces better results than trying to assume someone else's personality.

How do you structure your rehearsals?

On the high-school level I opened each rehearsal with the *Treasury of Scales,* one of the best warm-up books ever written. Next I selected technical exercises from several different books whose names I have forgotten. Detailed practice on some concert selection always was next. Then I tried to end each rehearsal with a short, snappy march to produce a final adrenaline rush.

With my university bands I discovered soon that many, if not most music majors did not need warm-ups; indeed, they may have already played their instruments all day. Therefore I tried to structure each rehearsal minute-by-minute to maintain a balance between excitement and musical repose. I tried to never get bogged down too long on a thorny musical problem. When no progress seemed to be made, I switched to a different piece of music immediately. My minute-by-minute rehearsal timetable, placed on the board each day, helped me to stay on track.

How do you approach score study?

I approach it cautiously, with fear, trepidation, and a sense of excitement and anticipation. I want to find out what I think is in the music, not just what I may hear on someone else's CD. I want to get into my head the sounds that I will try to coax from my musicians. I *must* have a full aural picture of what I want to hear before I give the first downbeat.

I have no particular system except to sit and stare at a score until I can hear what is in it. I sing parts, count rhythms, make whatever markings I believe are necessary to jog my memory when I go over the music again, and keep at it until my musical ideas seem to coalesce into a satisfactory musical blueprint.

What is your concept of band sound? How do you achieve it?

In the final analysis, effective band balance (or sound) *must exist* in the mind of the conductor before it is projected by musicians to the ears of the audience. If the conductor has not originated a stable concept of ideal balance in his head, the result is musical happenstance. Performance balance may be good (not often), it may be bad (usually), but it always will be by chance and never the same twice. However, it is *not* by chance that the finest bands, orchestras, and choruses sing the music to their respective audiences with clarity and excellent balance. It is invariably because the conductor guided the ensemble to this enviable goal.

It is not clear, when listening to some groups in concert, that their conductors understand the implications of the term balance—the word musicians use to describe the relative loudness of instruments in relationship to each other. If a firm concept of balance exists in the ear (mind) of every conductor, why are the results from one maestro to another so drastically different?

When listening to one band we hear only brass and percussion (plus an occasional *solo* or *tutti* woodwind passage when scored alone). With another group, a homogenous organ-like sound without variety emanates from the players most of the time. Some bands, especially when conducted by directors who bring the field band concept indoors, feature a percussion sound that is overbearing and a constant detriment to the music.

One conductor makes certain that soloists are heard at

all times; another covers up soloists with heavy accompaniments. When working with some conductors, brass musicians complain of never being able to play with a full tone. Others (woodwind players) say plaintively that they cannot be heard. Since there is so much variance in the basic sound of different groups, and the same group under various conductors, this variance can only be attributed to varying concepts of balance. Balance is affected by physical differences in the sensory organs associated with the hearing process or the control/lack of control exerted by the person on the podium.

Creating a good musical balance between individual performers and sections is the province of the conductor. Obviously the standpoint of conductor and performer are totally different. The performer hears *only* the sound of the surrounding players. The individual player is acutely aware (if she is a good, conscientious musician) of her stand partner, the general harmony or counterpoint of the neighboring parts, and the relative loudness of her own sound compared to others in the vicinity.

But this musician, no matter how good, cannot know whether specific sounds blend with the group as a whole (especially in a large group). That must be the province of the conductor, who is the only person in the central position necessary to hear and compare the relative strength of all parts. Therefore it stands to reason that the conductor is the one who has the responsibility to create the perfect balance between all the different parts that are competing for the attention of the audience.

How to define good balance? A list of objectives may be helpful:

1. The most important musical line must be heard clearly
    by the audience at all times.
    a. A musically defensible identification of the relative
        weight of all parts must be made by the conductor
        through prior score study.
    b. A clear identification of the relative importance of
        parts must be conveyed to the ensemble.
    c. The conductor must insist that performers follow
        the instructions given to them. Quite often this is
        the most neglected aspect in a rehearsal. It does no
        good for the conductor to recognize the fact that one
        section is too loud in relation to another if the louder
        section does not obey instructions to play softer.
2. There must be a woodwind presence at all times in *tutti*
    chords except in the most massive of *fortississimos,*
    where good woodwind balance is literally impossible
    to achieve. Otherwise, why would composers bother
    to write woodwind parts if they are not going to be
    heard when the brass and percussion parts are written
    above *mf*?
    a. Take into account the number of players in each
        of the three primary categories (woodwinds,
        brass, percussion) when setting balance between
        sections.
    b. Take into account the relative playing experience
        and dynamic capability of players in each category
        when setting balance between sections.
3. In homophonic music the principal melody should be
    supported by the accompaniment, not obliterated by
    it.
4. In contrapuntal music each new entrance must be heard
    clearly by the audience.

5. Bring melodies strongly to the front if the *tessitura* of the accompaniment is the same as or higher than the melody.

6. Good chordal balance on wind instruments can only be achieved by playing the lower parts of a chord progressively stronger than the upper parts, or higher parts softer than lower parts. Think of the relative weight of each note in a chord as if the dynamics are relative to the shape of a triangle, with each tone played slightly louder than the one above it.

7. Dynamic markings are for the audience, not necessarily for the performer. Play so that any musically knowledgeable member of the audience could describe the major dynamic markings in the score if asked to do so. In other words, a clarinet solo marked *pp* on the part should sound soft to listeners in the last row of the auditorium and not be inaudible to them. In order to achieve this musical goal, the performer, depending on the accompaniment, might have to play the part *mf* or louder.

8. The conductor must put himself mentally in the place of the audience and see that the composer's intentions are imparted to the listener (i.e., the audience hears and follows at all times the ideas of the composer, whatever they are).

9. What the conductor sees in the score should be heard by the audience, if scored well by the composer.

10. Re-score and re-balance by changing dynamics, if needed, to realize the composer's musical intentions.

11. Group or block dynamics (i.e., dynamics written the same in all parts must be interpreted by the conductor to conform to the relative dynamic weight of each instrument or section).

How does the beginning conductor develop the sixth sense necessary to guide musicians of any age to play with proper balance? It's simple: just *listen, listen, listen* to fine ensembles of all kinds on every level of performance with all types and styles of repertoire. Be eclectic. Don't *just* listen to band music; don't *just* listen to orchestra music; and don't *just* listen to jazz, or rock, or any one genre.

My ideas of balance were set by listening to (and playing in) the marvelous bands of William Revelli and Hugh McMillen. James Robertson, the orchestra director at Wichita University, also made a lasting impression on my young mind when I was fortunate enough to play under his baton. I went to every concert I could find (and afford), and still do. Basically this is how I learned whatever I know about balance. There are no shortcuts, nor should there be. This road is not arduous; it deals with the subject we all love: music.

Beware, however, of one pitfall brought on by our manipulative new recording technologies. Auditorium balance, and that of the many CDs now on the market are two different things. Most any instrumentation can be balanced perfectly with digital techniques, but these same ensembles may sound nothing like that when heard in person. In the everyday world we still must balance bands without the artificial aid of electronic volume controls. Our volume control *must* be in our heads, with the resulting balance conveyed to the ensemble through appropriate conducting gestures and comments.

What are your views on score marking?
Find each conducting problem, discover the correct solution, and *write the solution in the score* using your own individual markings. The marks should be easily visible when conducting from the podium. I mark my scores copiously because:

1. Well-done score annotating gives constant reminders as I review and conduct my scores.
2. I don't have to reinvent the wheel when I pull a score out again several years later.

Do mark your scores unless you have a photographic memory. In fact, annotation and singing are my methods of choice for score memorization. I used to have trouble with rental scores, but solved the problem with yellow stickies. In fact I use them often in my own scores to draw my eyes to a particular problem or solution.

Some conductors believe they do not need score markings for concert conducting. Actually, my main reason for *marking* a score is to *learn* the score and to *remember* what I learned at a later date.

How can we best advance our art?

We must show others how a love of music can enhance all lives whether or not it leads to a professional career. We must fight the battle of convincing our students that great musical ideas are more worthy of our attention than trivia. Constantly listening to trivial music wastes our time, surely one of the greatest sins in the world.

What works did you program on your farewell concert?

Traditionally, the last concert of the year featured both the Wind Ensemble (second band) and the Symphonic Band. As conductor of the Wind Ensemble, D. Robert Fleming chose his own program and soloists (not listed).

To open the second half of my final concert I chose to feature one of our fine faculty pianists, Walter Cosand, performing my wind arrangement of the *Concerto in D minor* by J. S. Bach (my *Desert Island* composer).

Next I chose to challenge the band and myself by programming all movements of the *Greek Dances* by Nikos Skalkottas (arranged by Gunther Schuller). I had never conducted this fascinating, extremely difficult work before, so I just decided to do it. The band loved it (after they had mastered its intricacies), and I cherished every rhythmic note and ethnic melodic line.

I invited Guido Six, a fine friend of mine from Belgium to come and guest-conduct a short, snappy original work: *Arlequino,* by Belgian composer Roland Cardon.

Finally, as I had ended every season since it was voted our National March, I played *The Stars and Stripes Forever* by John Phillip Sousa. Then (just because I wanted to do so), I conducted "America the Beautiful," one of my wife's favorite melodies. Nothing can follow that.

What are your current sources of inspiration or spiritual enrichment?

My wonderful family; listening to (studying) great music, now principally orchestral; purposeful reading; and reveling in the successful careers of my former students.

What are your interests beyond music?

Reading French, both classical (Dumas) and modern (Gide); medieval English history (my doctoral outside minor); travel; and photography.

To what do you attribute your exceptional musical success?

Whatever success I have had must be attributed to having latched onto exceptional teachers and mentors and having a large dose of *musical curiosity.*

If you could do it all over again, would you do anything differently?

I have always wondered what would have happened to my career if, at some point, I had concentrated on orchestral rather than band conducting. *Qui sait?* [Who knows?]

How would you like your epitaph to read?

I don't need an epitaph on my tombstone; I will just leave the stone blank, and the passer-by will say automatically, "That's Strange."

Any final thoughts or words of advice?

Do any of us truly remember what it was like to be a beginner in all phases of music, from reading notation to playing an instrument? For me, it seems so long ago that I cannot really revisit the thrill of producing those esoteric music symbols in sound, simple though the melodies were at the beginning by singing as a small child and later with instruments. The first few days and months spent learning to play an instrument produced only basic sounds and tunes. I took a breath when needed by the body, which was often, not when called for by a musical phrase. I was happy to hear a respectable tone from the instrument; the idea of adding dynamic variations to the sound came in a distant second.

Then, one day (if you were like me), our teacher told us, "Breathe after a long note, not before" for better musical phrasing. What a shock! I thought the right notes were all that were needed. That was hard enough without adding further complications. Fortunately, several excellent teachers insisted that I make music from the notes; unfortunately, the teachers of many students do not.

Nuance is easy to define in broad terms but difficult to put into practice. Let us first look at several dictionary definitions:

Nuance	Adopted from the French word for a difference, or shade, of meaning, feeling, opinion, or color. In a musical sense the word is used to describe the delicate differences of intensity and of speed which play a large part in giving life to music. (Denis Arnold, ed. *The New Oxford Companion to Music,* Vol. 2.)
Nuance (Fr.)	Shade, distinction, gradation. A word frequently used by writers on music to imply those delicate differences of intensity and speed which largely constitute the character of a performance. (Michael Kennedy. *The Oxford Dictionary of Music.*)
Nuances [F.]	Subtle modifications of intensity, tempo, touch, phrasing, etc... (Willi Apel, ed. *The Harvard Dictionary of Music,* 2nd ed.)

These succinct definitions are exact as far as they go but leave much to the imagination in terms of how to add interest to any given musical grouping of notes. The addition of nuance, in the smallest sense, has as its goal the creation of apparent movement from one note toward another to build each individual phrase and to produce a logical connection between phrases. This musical enhancement of each small section helps to create larger musical ideas in the mind of the listener and eliminate musical boredom.

To obtain these desirable results, both conductor and players should be able to identify motives, phrases, and longer musical periods having to do with formal structure. Yes, fellow conductors, those classes in history, theory, and form-and-analysis that you took in school were important after all!

Pity those musicians (?) who paid no attention in class and still pay no attention because they are too preoccupied with non-musical matters to care.

Here are a series of performance suggestions, some obvious, some not:

1. In terms of both tempo and dynamics, first follow the composer's notated directions. We have all heard performances during which the stated wishes of the composer were ignored completely. Why? If the composer's directions are on the printed page, use them unless you have an overriding musical reason for making a change. Musical laziness (inertia) is *not* a good reason.

2. Teach your students, even some advanced ones, that the choice of a spot for breathing is an integral part of turning a musical phrase, not just a convenience for the wind instrument player. In most music it is still good advice to breathe after the longest note of a phrase, not before. Naturally this rule must be modified at times for tubists and bass trombonists when playing long phrases.

3. Add implied dynamics when not written by the composer. In general, add a slight *crescendo* to most rising musical lines, and a slight *decrescendo* to most descending musical lines. When appropriate, this gives the feeling of constant, almost imperceptible, change that helps to preclude listener fatigue.

4. Enhance repeated notes on the same pitch by adding a *crescendo* toward the first non-repeated note unless the repeated notes constitute a long accompaniment figure. Pablo Casals felt that repetition in music, be it of a single note or of a phrase, is similar to repetition of words or phrases in speech. It is a natural feature of

expressive communication to vary the emphasis when we say the same thing more than once. For instance, reiterating "I love you" in a monotone will not get you very far with the opposite sex. Another case in point: in the last act of *King Lear*, the despairing monarch addresses the lifeless body of Cordelier:

> Thou'lt come no more,
> Never, never, never, never, never!

The first thing an actor instinctively realizes is that he must vary the force of intensity from one word to the next. He achieves repetition without duplication. "It is a general rule that repeated notes or a repeated design must not be equal," Casals reminded his students. "Something has to be done. Otherwise you have monotony, [I love this quote] and nothing is more monotonous than monotony!" "*Con amore—con amore,*" he urged, going over a particular phrase a dozen times, "otherwise it means nothing—it's against the music!

"Repetition in music means more *piano* or more *forte*—like when you are speaking; in music it's the same—give expression, and then more expression!" It didn't matter to Casals that most nuance was not marked in the score. "There are one thousand things that are not marked," he thundered. "Don't give notes; give the meaning of the notes!" (David Blum, *Casals and the Art of Interpretation.*)

5. When adding non-notated dynamics (see point three above), one must keep in mind the short phrase (motive) *in* the melody versus the long line of the melody. Usually, there should be only one *highest* point in the long line, although additional nuance can (and should) be added

if it does not overshadow the climax. What is appropriate; what is not? Only the ear of the experienced musician can tell.

6. Instrumental and vocal *timbre* is a part of nuance. Make tone quality fit the character of the music. *All* great artists do this.

7. Nuance also includes all slight changes of tempo not dictated by the composer: small hesitations [*tenuto*] and subtle pushing of tempo within measures that do not disturb the overall tempo. Most small nuances of tempo should cease at the bar line so as not to change the overall pace of the music, unless a *ritard* or *accelerando* is wanted or needed.

Casals said, "Time lost on expressive accents being placed on the first note of a group, or on the highest note, is to be regained by the intervening notes (before going to the next bar)."

Torsi expressed this same principle in his classic treatise, *Observations on the Florid Song...Useful for all Performers, Instrumental as well as Vocal* (John Ernest Galliard, trans., 1743): "The stealing of Time...is an honorable Theft in one that sings better than others, provided he makes a Restitution with Ingenuity."

A humorous aside: although the conductor sets non-notated nuances of tempo most of the time, this is not always true. I once conducted a series of Mozart's piano concertos with an intractable (but excellent) pianist who insisted there be no *ritard* before either cadenzas or the ends of movements. This went against all of my musical instincts and those of the excellent professional orchestra. I never was able to keep myself, or the orchestra members, from shading ending tempos with a slight *ritard*, much to the disgust of the pianist.

8. Most nuance should be SUBTLE (not like these capital letters), with slight gradations of lightness and darkness, figuratively speaking. Melodies and intertwining lines need to be built into readily discernable musical structures without assaulting the ears of the audience with overblown musical hysterics unless specifically called for by the composer.

9. Nuance should never be so subtle (see point six above) that it is not heard by the listener, regardless of the size of the auditorium or other listening space. Subtleties that do not reach the ear of the audience did not happen as far as the audience is concerned. Starting with the first note of a piece of music, interpretation (the adding of nuance) is all-important. When studying the illuminated manuscripts of the Middle Ages we are constantly amazed at the artistic beauty of the first letter of each paragraph, page, or chapter. Skilled calligraphers were engaged to embellish these letters in order to capture the imagination of the reader from the beginning.

For the same reason, never let even the first note of a solo or *tutti* passage in music escape the attention of the listener. The performer must give it an immediate sense of presence, with enough volume to push it out to the ear of the listener. If the passage before was loud, soft notes must still be projected to the audience. Casals said simply, "A *piano* following immediately on the heels of a *forte* will often sound too soft because of the sudden contrast in dynamics."

10. The group should echo nuance added to a solo line when repeating the solo phrase (or vice versa). "Whoever gets there first, wins" is a good rule to follow.

How to learn more about nuance? Easy! Just listen to the world's greatest artists, all of whom have many fine performances on CDs and tapes. Keep your radio tuned to local classical music FM stations and pay close attention to the finer details of musicality as displayed by each individual musician.

Concert band directors, no matter what they call their groups, have a readymade way to obtain CDs representing the finest of contemporary playing and conducting. All of the major service bands will help you to build a fine library of recordings for your band room. Just send a letter or facsimile on school stationary requesting to receive all releases and you will be flooded with excellent examples of style and nuance. What better way for students to learn the most esoteric principles of band sound and interpretation than to listen to the playing of the U. S. Marine Band, the U. S. Air Force Band, and all the others who so generously send their recordings to non-profit organizations and directors who ask. For addresses, just search the web and for the names of the various bands you want to hear.

However, for analytical purposes, it does no good just to let musical sound wash over you. You must listen carefully and catalogue all aspects of each interpretation for later use, when appropriate, in your own performances. A morsel here, a morsel there, and mysteriously, other people's ideas will enhance your own interpretations. My motto is: "Steal (borrow) only from the best!" To steal ideas from the best is not plagiarism. Imitation (the sincerest form of flattery) is the way the performers to whom you are listening learned from *their* teachers.

Indeed, speaking of borrowing from the best, one of my most powerful musical memories is of a two-week workshop given at Carnegie-Mellon University years ago by Pablo Casals. His musicianship was of an order that seemed light years above anyone else. This was immediately apparent to all of us who attended his master classes. I sincerely believe that I learned more about musical phrasing in those weeks than ever before or after. I still strive to use his simple principles in all of my music making to this day.

For instance, some musicians restrict and categorize the degree of expression that may be brought to the performance of music of the Baroque and Classical periods, but Casals was not a person to withhold nuance from any musical interpretation. He did not undervalue the depth of feeling with which our ancestors experienced the music they composed and performed. He understood that musicians living in the seventeenth and eighteenth centuries did not regard their art as historic; it was a living event.

Mozart wrote:

> Would you like to know how I have expressed and even indicated the beating, loving heart? By two violins playing octaves.... You feel the trembling—the faltering—you see how the throbbing breast begins to heave; this I have indicated by a crescendo. You hear the whispering and the sighing...

In this, Mozart showed himself to be a true son of his father, for Leopold Mozart once wrote: "It is as clear as sunlight that every effort must be made to put the player in the mood which reigns in the piece itself, in order thereby to penetrate the souls of the listeners and to excite their emotions" (David Blum, *Casals and the Art of Interpretation*).

Concerning the proper performance of Johann Sebastian Bach's music, there are two diametrically opposed schools of thought with every possible shading in between. To state the obvious, contemporary ideas of performance practice range from "just play the notes and let the music stand on its own" to "add as much nuance as possible." I must say that I tend toward the second view, as exemplified by the performances of Bach's music by Casals. It is inconceivable to me that one of the world's greatest musicians would not have added a large amount of nuance to his own music when he conducted or supervised its performance and added subtle tempo changes when playing the organ. In other words, I cannot believe that Bach just ground his music out by the pound.

In Bach's era, musicians wrote most compositions for their own use and did not feel the need to take the extra time necessary to add a great number of expressive markings. Obviously they expected to be at most (if not all) rehearsals and performances, so the music was under their personal control. Presumably they already knew how they wanted the music to sound—after all, they wrote it. What would we not give for a recording of Bach, playing or conducting his own music!

I must recommend a paperback book that should be in the library of every fine musician. The words of great musicians allow us to understand, to a certain degree, the thinking behind their performances. However, many of the world's greatest composers and performers provided very few written explanations of their musical ideas, leaving that task to their disciples.

Just as Stravinsky had his Robert Kraft, so, also, Casals had an amanuensis: David Blum. Blum collected Casals' musical thoughts and ideas as others might collect butterflies and put them into book form. After one becomes inured to Blum's fawning attitude toward his subject, *Casals and the*

Art of Interpretation is must reading. I have included a distillation comprised of quotations and my own paraphrases of a few of Blum's gleanings from many of the performances and clinics given by Casals.

The few tidbits given above should whet your appetite for more of the musical thoughts of Pablo Casals concerning nuance and the interpretation of music. As a band director, don't be afraid to learn from the masters of the orchestral world. Great musical ideas transcend artificial boundaries raised by words such as band, orchestra, chorus, wind ensemble, etc.

Every page of Blum's book contains suggestions from Casals that can change or reinforce your musical ideas forever. Any bookstore should be able to order this wonderful compendium of ideas for you by using the following information:

> Blum, David. *Casals and the Art of Interpretation.* Berkeley, CA: University of California Press, 1977. ISBN: 0-520-04032-5.

David Blum placed the following words in Pablo Casals' mouth: "The art of interpretation is *not* to play what is written." In these words, Casals stated a fundamental tenet of his music making. He implied that written notes give the musician only a rough guide to the content of the music. The fine musician *adds* feeling, clarity, movement, and purpose to the written phrase to make it come alive to the listener. An overriding concern when adding nuance to a phrase, is, "Does it work?" "That's beautiful, isn't it?" said Casals, when demonstrating a passage during a master class at Carnegie-Mellon University when I was in attendance. "Well, if it's beautiful, it's good."

The average musician plays for herself. In other words,

she just plays the notes. The finest musician *communicates* musical ideas to others without descending into caricatures of the musical intent of the composer. This musician creates, and sometimes overdoes (a little), the implied nuance so as to connect with the audience.

Virtuosity on any level is much more than just the mastery of the notes. It is the ability to project the innate logic of the music, which is almost never completely notated. Although Stravinsky states that his music should be performed just as written with nothing added, even he did not adhere to this silly pronouncement when conducting his own works with the finest professional performers.

Nuance, then, is the realization and projection of the *implications* inherent in the music. Many times these implications become clear only after years of study and are not obvious, even to the composer, when first written and performed. I have come to the empirical conclusion, based on a lifetime of listening to recordings made at different stages in each performer's professional life, that the interpretations of well-known music by famous musicians grows more romantic and intuitive as the performers age. In general, tempos slow down, more nuance is added, and musical intuition plays a larger part in the interpretation.

A case in point: Yo-Yo Ma and the Bach *Cello Suites*. The performance on these CDs represents the application of nuance in its purest form. Yo-Yo Ma, a master performer, takes the composer's raw material and shapes it with the highest level of musical imagination to project the implications contained in the written notes. Instead of sounding sterile (as happens in many cello recitals), the music of Bach comes alive because of the fertile imagination of the consummate artist. I have listened to these marvelous performances over and over and have learned again that there is no limit to the musical imagination of a fine performer when playing the inspired creations of one of the world's greatest composers. Do I sound like a Yo-Yo Ma/Bach groupie? You bet! This is the way I learn and enjoy at the same time.

Another case in point: In later years, when performing the *Courante* from the Bach *Third Suite*, Casals lightened the texture of the descending *arpeggios* by playing them off the string in *diminuendo*. "The purists are scandalized because I do that," he said, adding sardonically: "because it seems—*it seems*—that in Bach's time staccato didn't exist. But don't be afraid."

As was often the case, Casals, by trusting his own intuition, came to conclusions which were later supported by musico-logical research. It is now known that *staccato* and *spiccato* bowings were employed by such eighteenth-century virtuosi as Tartini and Geminiani. As early as 1687 Jean Rousseau, in his *Trite de la Viole*, referred to the frequent use of rebounding bow strokes which are called *ricochets*.

However, be careful! Herbert von Karajan became so willful in his interpretations at times that rests in the slow sections of some of the symphonies he recorded have no discernable rhythm whatsoever, especially if one tries to count through a repeated series of rests. He simply ignored the time and started the next entrance when he pleased. (Listen to his interpretation of the opening of Tchaikovsky's *Symphony no. 5* with the Berlin Philharmonic Orchestra). He got away with it. Lesser mortals (such as you and I) would have been laughed off the stage by the musicians.

Once in a while age lends so much perspective that conductors have been known to slow tempos almost to the point of lugubriousness. Bruno Walter, in his final years, was asked by Columbia Records to record all nine symphonies of Beethoven with a specially chosen group of Los Angeles musicians called the Columbia Symphony Orchestra. His tempos were so slow, and the interpretations were so packed with an excessive amount of nuance that the set disappeared from view shortly thereafter.

Many composers and performers throughout history other than the ones quoted above have made comments about interpretation. The following statements all represent ideas already put forth:

"Music," Claude Debussy once famously remarked, "is the stuff between the notes."

Just before the premiere of *The Ring*, Richard Wagner issued a last request in a handwritten note to the singers:

> !Clarity!
> The big notes come of themselves; it is little notes that require attention...

Don't forget jazz! A listen to Doc Severinson playing with his *avant-garde* group Xebron reveals the very best of jazz nuance (*Doc Severinson & Xebron*, Passport 88008)! Artie Shaw's famous clarinet solo on the old standard "Stardust" is a great example of the use of nuance to build excitement. Stan Kenton, in his albums entitled *Sketches on Standards*, started softly and built wonderful climaxes on such tunes as "There's a Small Hotel" and others.

Young directors can add contemporary examples to underline the same principles. In other words, don't just play everything louder, faster, and higher in the name of Jazz. Subtlety *à la* Miles Davis goes much further to make musical points than using only sheer adrenaline. Pauses, silence, deliberateness, contrast, inventiveness, and a long list of other nuances are what jazz is made of.

Heartfelt and logical nuance makes any set of notes sound better. Use it carefully and wisely, but use it always.

'

Chapter 9

DAVID WHITWELL

How did you begin your musical journey? Who were your first teachers and sources of inspiration?

First, my mother, who emphasized the communication of emotion in music. Second, my first instrumental teacher, who charged no fee, but charged five cents per mistake.

Were there any conductors who made a lasting impression on you during your early years?

Fritz Reiner, Bruno Walter, Eugene Ormandy, Leopold Stokowski, Leonard Bernstein, George Solti, and Herbert von Karajan. I have had the opportunity to hear these men conduct many times. The last five I have had the opportunity to talk with privately and discuss music and performance practice.

If you could begin your college years all over again, would you do anything differently?

I would not be a music education major. For anyone interested in conducting or in music education, the critical thing in these valuable years is to become a good musician. What is taught in music education classes is neither about music nor education.

What advice can you offer to current music majors or young band directors?

Every day you must remind yourself that you are an artist. If you are a conductor, even at the elementary level, you must remind yourself you are an artist-conductor. This is crucial for two reasons:

1. Maintaining your self-image as an artist is the foundation for well being. If you allow yourself to become an entertainer, or your primary identification is as a music educator, as a musician you will be haunted with a lack of self-respect.

2. If you do not work as an artist, you will work below the level of your students, even at the elementary school level. Since the most important aspects of music are genetic, even fifth graders understand what is important in music. Students of any age become quickly bored if you work beneath their level. Never underestimate such children. I once had the opportunity to hear a performance by a grade-school orchestra of the last movement of Tchaikovsky's Symphony no. 4. The entire orchestra played *by memory!*

How do you structure your rehearsals?

I plan rehearsals over several weeks to guarantee appropriate distribution of rehearsal time. Since I rehearse without scores, the pace is very fast. I focus entirely on musical solutions.

I have found that on the average there are two hours of thinking time for each hour of rehearsal. Thus, a two-hour rehearsal requires four hours of reflection, before and after rehearsal. Since scores are memorized, none of this time has to do with score study.

How do you approach score study?

My goal is to understand the feeling the composer was feeling. The only sure way that I have found to do this is by memorization of the score in order to be able to hear the music without the interference of the eye, which tends to be attracted only to the grammar of the composition. The memorization system I use is actually a European system of score study based on a different kind of form than is taught in our schools. To my knowledge, all important conductors have used some version of this system.

What is your concept of band sound? How do you achieve it?

There is a natural sound based on the overtone series for a band, and it is very much like an organ sound. Careful pyramiding (less top, more bottom) is always necessary to overcome the natural tendency for the brain to boost upper partials, beginning with third-space C in the treble clef.

How can we best advance our art?

We must be artists and not entertainers. The concert band is a very poor medium for entertainment.

What works did you program on your farewell concert?

California State University, Northridge Wind Ensemble, May 5, 2000.

Richard Wagner	*Overture to Reinzi*
David Whitwell	Symphony no. 1
Hardy Martens	*U Mundu Drentu A Ti*
Yasuhide Ito	*Gururiyoza*
Strauss	*Also Sprach Zarathustra*
Percy Grainger	*Irish Tune*

What are your current sources of inspiration or spiritual enrichment?

The music I am studying or hearing.

What are your interests beyond music?

American history, European history, fine literature, fine arts.

To what do you attribute your exceptional musical success?

Finding repertoire that communicates feeling to the audience.

How would you like your epitaph to read?

This person wasted too much time!

[For additional thoughts or words of advice, please investigate the excellent collection of Whitwell's essays at www.whitwellessays.com—Ed.]

Reading Lists

One of the many remarkable threads of commonality among all of the conductors featured in *The Conductor's Legacy* is that they never cease to learn. Their intellectual curiosity remains a vital part of their lives, even in retirement. Each was encouraged to share a selected reading list.

Not all books listed are about music. These titles may serve not only to enlighten the musician but also to rekindle the human spirit.

For all those who love to read, the following lists will provide reaffirmation of those books previously read and hopefully send the reader on a quest to enjoy those yet to be discovered.

Frank Battisti

Blum, David ....*Casals and the Art of Interpretation*

Copland, Aaron ....*Music and Imagination*

Foss, Lukas ....*A Twentieth-century Composer's Confessions about the Creative Process*

Gaskin, Elliott W. ....*A History of Orchestral Conducting: In Theory and Practice*

Grosbayne, Benjamin ....*Techniques of Modern Orchestral Conducting*

Herter Norton, MD ....*The Art of String Quartet Playing: Practice, Technique, and Interpretation*

Jacobson, Bernard ....*Conductors on Conducting*

Kohn, Elfie ....*No Contest: The Case against*
  Competition

Leinsdorf, Erich ....*The Composer's Advocate*

Prausnitz, Frederic ....*Score and Podium: A Complete Guide*
  to Conducting

Schuller, Gunther ....*Musings: The Musical Worlds of*
  Gunther Schuller

Sherman, Russell.......................*Piano Pieces*

Solti, Georg ....*Memoirs*

Wager, Jeannine ....*Conductors in Conversation*

Walter, Bruno ....*Of Music and Music Making*

Ray E. Cramer

  The Holy Bible

Battisti, Frank............................*The Winds of Change*

Bernstein, Leonard ....*The Joy of Music*

Bird, John ....*Percy Grainger*

Dungy, Tony ....*Quiet Strength*

Fennell, Frederick ....*The Wind Ensemble*

Goldman, Richard Franco ....*The Wind Band*

Green, Barry.............................*The Inner Game of Music*

....*The Mastery of Music*

Green, Elizabeth........................*The Modern Conductor* (all editions)

....*Practicing Successfully: A Master*
  Class in the Musical Art

Hansen, Richard ....*The American Wind Band—A Cultural*
  Revolution

Jacob, Arnold ....*The Legacy of a Master*

Jordan, James ....*The Musician's Soul*

Parker, Alice.............................*The Anatomy of Melody*

Ross, Alex ....*The Rest Is Noise*

Quindlen, Anna ....*A Short Guide to a Happy Life*

Walter, Bruno ....*Of Music and Music Making*

James Croft

Rather than burdening the reader with an extensive list of resources, many of which may well be redundant, I share with you references that have had significance for me. Some are practical, others theoretical, and all were and remain helpful. They, along with hundreds of volumes that repose in my library, include many that are used only occasionally, some that have not received much attention, and some that simply take up space. I call this my Sweet Sixteen list, and all are worth reading!

Sweet Sixteen

Battisti, Frank......................*The Winds of Change*
Bird, John.................................*Percy Grainger*
Dart, Thurston ....*The Interpretation of Music*
Dewey, John ....*Art as Experience*
Dorian, Frederick ....*History of Music In Performance*
Gaskin, Elliot ....*The History of Orchestral Conducting*
Hanson, Richard......................*The American Wind Band*
Langer, Suzanne ....*Philosophy in a New Key*
Leinsdorf, Eric ....*The Composer's Advocate*
Meyer, Leonard ....*Emotion and Meaning in Music*
Reimer, Bennett ....*A Philosophy of Music Education*
Rogers, Carl ....*On Becoming*
Schuller, Gunther ....*The Compleat Conductor*
Thurmond, James....................*Note Grouping*
Wagner, Richard......................*On Conducting*
Walter, Bruno ....*On Music and Music Making*

My Sweet Sixteen list omits a number of very valuable references on pedagogy, policy, and procedure; many texts related to the teaching of conducting, the history and practice of instrumental performance, theory and analysis, and orchestration and literature. Time and space just doesn't permit these entries.

Ten Books That Made a Difference

Audrey, Robert ....*The Social Contract*

Boorstein, Daniel ....*The Discoverers*

Borowski, J. ....*On the Ascent of Man*

Gibran, Khalil ....*The Prophet*

Gladwel, Malcolm.....................*Blink*

Hoofer, Eric..............................*The True Believer*

Matheopolous, Helena ....*Maestro*

McCollough, David....................*John Adams*

Neill, A. S. ....*Summerhill*

Schuller, Gunther ....*Musings*

Col. Arnald Gabriel

Ambrose, Stephen ....*Citizens Soldiers*

Band of Brothers

D-Day: June 6, 1944

Borge, Victor.............................*My Favorite Comedies in Music*

Brokaw, Tom ....*The Greatest Generation*

Brown, Dan ....*The Da Vinci Code*

Brown, Rosemary ....*Unfinished Symphonies*

Camphouse, Mark, ed. ....*Composers on Composing for Band*, vols. I–IV

Chopra, Deepak.........................*Quantum Healing*

Eisenhower, Dwight D...............*Soldier and President*

Gillis, Don................................*The Unfinished Symphony Conductor*

Grisham, John ....*Playing for Pizza*

Hull, Gene ....*Hooked on Horns*

Kozak, Warren ....*LeMay: The Life and Wars of Curtis LeMay*

Kriegel, Mark ....*Pistol*

Jacobs, Arnold ....*Song and Wind*

Lewis, Michael ....*The Blind Side*

Previn, Andre ....*Orchestra*

Reiss, Alvin ....*Cash In!*

Sachs, Harvey ....*Toscanini*

Schuller, Gunther ....*The Compleat Conductor*

Waitley, Denis ....*The Psychology of Winning*

Wallace, David ....*Life In the Balance*

Walsh, Neale Donald.................*Friendship With God*

Weintraub, Stanley ....*Fifteen Stars*

Wilson, Meredith ....*And There I Stood With My Piccolo*

Zander, Rosamund and

    Benjamin ....*The Art of Possibilities*

H. Robert Reynolds

Battisti, Frank, and

    Robert Garofalo...................*Guide to Score Study for the Wind Band Conductor*

Battisti, Frank............................*The Twentieth-century American Wind Band Ensemble: History, Development and Literature*

Cipolla, Frank J. and

    D. Hunsberger ....*The Wind Ensemble and Its Repertoire: Essays on the Fortieth Anniversary of the Eastman Wind Ensemble*

Cott, Jonathan ....*Conversations with Glenn Gould*

Elliot, David J. ....*Music Matters: A New Philosophy of Music Education*

Fennell, Frederick ....*Time and the Winds*

Furlong, William Barry ....*Season with Solti: A Year in the Life of the Chicago Symphony*

Holden, Raymond ....*The Virtuoso Conductors*

Kenyon, Nicholas ....*Simon Rattle from Birmingham to Berlin*

Kohn, Elfie ....*No Contest: The Case Against*
Competition

Lebrecht, Norman ....*The Maestro Myth: Great Conductors*
in Pursuit of Power

Leinsdorf, Erich ....*The Composer's Advocate: A Radical*
Orthodoxy for Musicians

Muscleman, Joseph A. ....*Dear People...Robert Shaw: A*
Biography

Ross, Alex ....*The Rest is Noise*

Slonimsky, Nicolas ....*Lexicon of Musical Invective: Critical*
Assaults on Composers since
Beethoven's Time

Vaughan, Roger..........................*Herbert von Karajan: A Biographical*
Portrait

Winter, Rodney ....*An Annotated Guide to Wind Chamber*
Music

While all books listed above are important, those which follow are especially meaningful to me.

Adolphe, Bruce ....*What to Listen for in the World*

Blum, David ....*Casals and the Art of Interpretation*

Casey, Joseph L ....*Teaching Techniques and Insights (for*
Instrumental Music Educators)

Henley, Fritz ....*Casals* (photographs and quotes)

Jordan, James ....*The Musician's Soul*
The Musician's Walk

Myers, Tona Pearce, ed. ....*The Soul of Creativity*

Walter, Bruno ....*Of Music and Music Making*

Zander, Rosamund and
Benjamin ....*The Art of Possibility*

CONTRIBUTORS

Frank Battisti

Frank Battisti is Conductor Emeritus of the New England Conservatory Wind Ensemble, which he founded and conducted for thirty years. The NEC Wind Ensemble is recognized as being one of the premiere ensembles of its kind in the United States and throughout the world.

Battisti has been responsible for commissioning and premiering over fifty works for wind ensemble by distinguished American and foreign composers. Critics, composers, and colleagues have praised Battisti for his commitment to contemporary music and his outstanding performances.

He is Past President of the College Band Directors National Association (CBDNA), a member of the American Bandmasters Association (ABA), and founder of the National Wind Ensemble Conference, World Association of Symphonic Bands and Ensembles (WASBE), Massachusetts Youth Wind Ensemble (MYWE) and New England College Band Association (NECBA).

Battisti constantly contributes articles on wind ensemble/band literature, conducting and music education to journals and magazines and is considered one of the foremost authorities in the world on wind music literature. In 2000 he was appointed the inaugural conductor for the Tanglewood Institute's Young Artists Wind Ensemble.

Col. John Bourgeois

Director Emeritus Colonel John R. Bourgeois, USMC (Ret.), was the twenty-fifth director of "The President's Own" United States Marine Band. His acclaimed career spanned nine presidential administrations, from Presidents Dwight D. Eisenhower to Bill Clinton.

Bourgeois is a graduate of Loyola University in New Orleans. He joined the Marine Corps in 1956 and entered "The President's Own" as a French hornist and arranger in 1958. Named Director of the Marine Band in 1979, Bourgeois was promoted to colonel in June 1983. He retired from active duty July 11, 1996.

Among the many honors and awards Bourgeois has received are the 1986 Phi Beta Mu Outstanding Bandmaster Award and the 1987 Kappa Kappa Psi Distinguished Service to Music Award for "contributions to the growth and development of modern college and university bands." In 1993 he was awarded the Midwest International Band and Orchestra Clinic Medal of Honor. Bourgeois was elected to the Academy of Wind and Percussion Artists of the National Band Association in 1988 and received the 1991 Phi Mu Alpha Sinfonia National Citation "for service and dedication to music and country."

Since retiring from the Marine Band, Col. Bourgeois has been actively involved in music as a guest conductor, has published new editions of classic band compositions, and is a visiting professor in a chair endowed in his name at Loyola University in New Orleans.

Ray E. Cramer

It is a long distance from rural western Illinois to the great concert halls of the world, but Ray Cramer has, in a remarkable career of music-making and teaching, experienced that adventure, and in the process touched the lives of countless numbers of musicians. Over the years at Indiana University he has done it all—everything from conducting the IU Big Red Pep Band in Assembly Hall to conducting the University Orchestra for annual productions of the ballet *The Nutcracker.*

After earning his MFA in 1963, Ray taught for two years in West Liberty, Iowa, where he was the band director of every grade—elementary, middle school, and high school. All of his groups were successful, earning top ratings at various festivals.

When Frederick Ebbs retired as chair of the Indiana University Department of Music in 1982, Ray Cramer was appointed as director of bands after a national search was completed. During his tenure the Indiana University Wind Ensemble performed at prestigious music conventions and conferences, earning a reputation as one of, if not the finest, collegiate wind ensembles in the world.

Ray has conducted the wind ensemble at the Musachino Academy of Music in Tokyo, one of the largest collegiate music schools in the world.

In retirement Ray continues to guest-conduct all-state bands, intercollegiate bands, and other groups, filling his schedule with much music-making and travel. He has guest-conducted nearly every one of the fifty all-state bands in the last twenty-five years.

—Submitted by Stephen Pratt

James Croft

James Croft, Emeritus Professor of Music Education and former Director of Bands at The Florida State University, received a BME from Cornell College (1951) an MA from Northern Iowa University (1955) and his doctorate from the University of Oklahoma (1970). Croft taught for twenty-one years in the public schools of Iowa and Wisconsin, where his groups were invited to appear at numerous state, regional, and national conventions, clinics and festivals. In 1972 he joined the faculty of the University of South Florida as Director of Bands, remaining there until moving to FSU in 1980.

Croft has appeared as a guest conductor, lecturer, adjudicator and/or clinician in forty-six states, throughout Europe, Brazil, Great Britain, Mexico, Canada, Israel and Australia. A Past President of both the National Band Association and the College Band Director's National Association, he has served as a Consulting Editor for *Research Perspectives in Music Education,* as a Contributing Editor for *The Instrumentalist* where he remains on the board of advisors, and is a frequent contributor to professional magazines, journals, and books.

Croft has been especially active as a champion of new music for the wind band, commissioning and/or premiering forty-seven world premiers and numerous American premiers.

Col. Arnald Gabriel

Col. Arnald D. Gabriel (USAF Ret.) retired from the United States Air Force in 1985 following a distinguished thirty-six-year career. He served as Commander/Conductor of the internationally known U. S. Air Force Band, Symphony Orchestra, and Singing Sergeants from 1964 to 1985. In February of 1990, Col. Gabriel was named the first Conductor Emeritus of the U. S. Air Force Band at a special concert at DAR Constitution Hall in Washington DC. One of the world's most widely traveled conductors, he has conducted bands and orchestras in all fifty of the United States and in forty-nine countries around the world.

Col. Gabriel revitalized the USAF Band's mission as America's International Musical Ambassadors by organizing two of the most outstanding foreign tours in the unit's then twenty-seven-year history; a twenty-six-concert Latin American tour of the USAF Band and Singing Sergeants in 1968 and a European tour in 1970 by the Band, Singing Sergeants, and the USAF Pipe Band, both greeted by wildly enthusiastic audiences numbering in the hundreds of thousands.

Col. Gabriel continues to appear as guest conductor, clinician, and adjudicator at major state, regional, and university music festivals across the country and conducts outstanding school, college, municipal, and military bands, as well as professional orchestras around the world.

H. Robert Reynolds

Following twenty-six years as Director of Bands at The University of Michigan, H. Robert Reynolds is now the principal conductor of the Wind Ensemble at the University of Southern California's Thornton School of Music, where he holds a professorship in his name. He has conducted the Detroit Chamber Winds and Strings (made up primarily of members from the Detroit Symphony) for over twenty-five years.

Professor Reynolds is Past President of the College Band Directors National Association and the Big Ten Band Directors Association. He has received the highest national awards from Phi Mu Alpha, Kappa Kappa Psi, the National Band Association, and the American School Band Directors Association, and he was awarded the Medal of Honor by the Midwest Band and Orchestra Clinic. He is the recipient of a

Special Tribute from the legislature of the State of Michigan signed by the leaders of the House, Senate and the Governor. Currently he is one of three members serving on the National Awards Panel for the American Society of Composers, Authors and Publishers (ASCAP), and in 2001 he received a national award from this organization for his contributions to contemporary American music.

Richard Strange

Dr. Richard E. Strange received degrees from Wichita University, the University of Colorado, and Boston University (a DMA in Performance). In Boston, he studied flute with George Madsen and clarinet with Pasquale Cardillo, both members of the Boston Symphony Orchestra. He served as Professor of Music and Director of Bands at Arizona State University for twenty-five years, and now holds the title of Director of Bands, Emeritus.

Active in the community orchestra field, Dr. Strange is currently in his thirty-fourth year as Music Director and Conductor of the Tempe Symphony Orchestra.

In recent years he has conducted, judged or given clinics in Austria, Belgium, Canada, England, France, Germany, Guam, Italy, Japan, The Netherlands, New Zealand, Sweden, Switzerland and the United States.

Dr. Strange is a Past President of the American Bandmasters Association and Executive Director of the American Bandmasters Association Foundation. He is also a Past President of the College Band Directors National Association.

David Whitwell

David Whitwell is a graduate with distinction of the University of Michigan and the Catholic University of America, Washington DC (PhD, Musicology and the Distinguished Alumni Award in 2000) and has studied conducting with Eugene Ormandy and at the Akademie fur Musik, Vienna. Dr. Whitwell participated in concerts throughout the United States and Asia as Associate First Horn in the USAF Band and Orchestra in Washington DC, and in recitals throughout South America in cooperation with the U. S. State Department.

At California State University, Northridge, Dr. Whitwell developed the CSUN Wind Ensemble into an ensemble of international reputation, with international tours to Europe in 1981 and 1989 and to Japan in 1984.Dr. Whitwell has been a guest professor in 100 different universities and conservatories throughout the United States and in twenty-three foreign countries.

He is a Past President of the College Band Directors National Association, a member of the Presidium of the International Society for the Promotion of Band Music, and was a member of the founding board of directors of the World Association for Symphonic Bands and Ensembles (WASBE).

Dr. Whitwell's publications include more than 115 articles on wind literature, including publications in *Music and Letters* (London), *The London Musical Times*, *The Mozart-Jahrbuch* (Salzburg), and thirty-eight books, among which is his thirteen-volume *History and Literature of the Wind Band Ensemble* and an eight-volume series on *Aesthetics in Music*. In addition to numerous modern editions of early wind band music his original compositions include five symphonies.

ABOUT THE EDITOR

Following a distinguished thirty-three-year teaching career, Professor **Paula A. Crider** continues to share her passion for making music through an active schedule as guest conductor, lecturer, clinician, and adjudicator. She has enjoyed engagements in forty-seven states, Canada, Ireland, the United Kingdom, France, Italy, and Australia. She is Professor Emerita at The University of Texas, where she was twice awarded the Eyes of Texas Award for distinguished teaching.

Professor Crider has taught at all levels of education, has presented seminars for professional teachers throughout the United States, and continues to work with talented young people in student leadership workshops. She serves as Coordinator for the National Band Association Young Conductor/Mentor Program and was recently appointed to the Conn/Selmer Educational Board.

She is a Past President of the National Band Association and is currently President Elect of the American Bandmaster's Association.